WORLDS *within* US

Worlds *within* Us

Wisdom and Resilience of Indigenous Women Elders

Edited by Katsi Cook
With Randi Barreiro and José Barreiro

Copyright © 2024 by Spirit Aligned Leadership Program / Rockefeller Philanthropy Advisors
Text copyright © 2021 by authors

All rights reserved. No part of this book may be reproduced or transmitted in any form whatsoever without the written permission of the publisher except in the case of brief quotations embodied in critical articles and reviews.

Published by Guaní™ Press for Spirit Aligned Leadership Program,
a sponsored project of Rockefeller Philanthropy Advisors, Inc.
Guaní Press, 109 Echo Hill Rd, Saugerties, NY 12477
For more information visit www.spiritaligned.org or www.guanipress.com

First Paperback Edition 2025

Cover image "The Rise of the Gray-Haired Women" © 2017 by Gayle Sinclaire, used by permission.

All photos used by permission of the individual copyright holders.
Cover portrait of editor © Nicole Jock Tuper
Portraits of authors pages 14, 46, 76, 98, 122, 154, 184, 214 © Nicole Jock Tuper
Portraits of authors pages 43, 72, 95, 151, 182 © Matika Wilbur • www.matikawilbur.com

Page 35, Dr. Henrietta Mann with Al Gore © 2007 The National Museum of the American Indian

Photos from the author's collections used by permission.
Dr. Henrietta Mann: pages 22, 26, 36, 40, 41; Loretta Afraid of Bear Cook: page 48;
Wakérakats:te Louise Herne: page 83; Nora Naranjo-Morse: pages 101, 103, 105, 108, 113, 115, 116, 119;
Jan Kahehti:io Longboat: pages 125, 128, 133; Sarah James: pages 158, 172, 178, 179, 181;
Yvonne Dupuis Peterson: pages 192, 199; Barbara Poley: pages 216, 222, 224, 230, 236

Design by Anabel Alfonso
Project Managing Editors: Raquel Picayo & Mario Picayo

Library of Congress Cataloging-in-Publication Data

Names: Cook, Katsi, editor. | Barreiro, Randi, editor. | Barreiro, José, editor.
Title: Worlds within Us : Wisdom and Resilience of Indigenous Women Elders / edited by Katsi Cook with Randi Barreiro and José Barreiro.
Description: New York : Spirit Aligned Leadership Program, 2024. | Includes index. |
Identifiers: LCCN 2023023722 (print) | LCCN 2023023723 (ebook) | ISBN 9781934370957 (paperback) | ISBN 9781934370971 (hardcover) | ISBN 9781934370988 (kindle edition)
Subjects: LCSH: Indian women elders (Indigenous leaders)--Biography. | LCGFT: Biographies.
Classification: LCC E89 .W895 2023 (print) | LCC E89 (ebook) | DDC 305.48/8970922 [B]--dc23/eng/20230607
LC record available at https://lccn.loc.gov/2023023722
LC ebook record available at https://lccn.loc.gov/2023023723

Printed in the United States of America

9 8 7 6 5 4 3 2 1

We dedicate this book and the lives it presents to the memory of our sister and martyr, Ingrid Washinawatok, Flying Eagle Woman (1957-1999), and to the memory of her life partner, Ali El-Issa, who followed her into the Spirit World in Fall 2022. We salute the activism that works from "love of the people," the commitment that deeply guides their lives.

Contents

Foreword — XI

Introduction — 3

Dr. Henrietta Mann — 13

Loretta Afraid of Bear Cook — 45

Wakérakats:te Louise Herne — 75

Nora Naranjo-Morse — 97

Jan Kahehti:io Longboat — 121

Sarah James — 153

Yvonne Dupuis Peterson — 183

Barbara Poley — 213

Afterword — 241

Acknowledgments — 247

1 Dr. Henrietta Mann
Southern Cheyenne

2 Loretta Afraid of Bear Cook
Oglala Lakota

3 Wakérakats:te Louise Herne
Akwesasne Mohawk

4 Nora Naranjo-Morse
Kha'p'o Owenge

5 Jan Kahehti:io Longboat
Kanien'kehá:ka – Six Nations of the Grand River

6 Sarah James
Neets'aii Gwich'in

7 Yvonne Dupuis Peterson
Chehalis

8 Barbara Poley
Laguna/Hopi

Foreword
THEY KNOW WHERE THEY ARE GOING

It is truly a miracle that we are here in this place and time, sharing the lives of these brave-hearted Indigenous women leaders.

They know where they are going. They manifest a better future and have dedicated their entire lives to creating a loving and balanced world.

This is truly remarkable, given what they have endured as the first peoples of this land.

Henrietta Mann shares the story of her mother sitting under the kitchen table rubbing the bullet wound in the leg of her grandmother from the Sand Creek Massacre. Henrietta is alive because her grandmothers "got away" from a massacre where soldiers cut fetuses from the wombs and later paraded through Denver with saddle horn covers and hat bands made from Cheyenne men's and women's genitalia.

Their stories may be hard to read for some, and their history is not included in school books. Indeed, our lives and our history are much more than what one reads in the history books.

Healing and forgiveness are centered in each woman's life. If they can heal and forgive, the rest of the world should at least know their stories…and learn from them.

FOREWORD

This book is like a tribal giveaway ceremony, where one honors the courageous life of each elder woman while collectively "making meaning" of their life. This is the reciprocal process of being invited to listen and learn from tribal elders.

When Sarah James shares her knowledge of climate migration by telling of the new animals and birds arriving in Arctic Village, her profound message is "they are welcome here." Sarah's next teaching is that "we don't hunt around the village so the caribou and other animals around us feel safe."

As human beings, we interpret what we hear from the context of our individual experiences. As such, sometimes we cannot relate to what we hear because it seems so far removed from our individual lives. Reading this book, I urge you to open your senses to the beautiful knowledge that comes from this land and its first peoples.

As Indigenous matriarchs, our source of strength is the love and knowledge that we have been given by our grandmothers. "I hope when it is my time to meet my great-grandmother Voestaa'e again, I can look her in the face and say I did my best," states Henrietta Mann.

We give thanks for the lives of these brave-hearted women. They are good teaching relatives to us all. To inspire future generations in truth and love is the hope of this book.

By Gail Small

Head Chief Woman, Northern Cheyenne
Program Director, Spirit Aligned Leadership Program

Worlds *within* Us

Introduction

ON BEHALF OF THEIR PEOPLES: CONSCIOUSNESS OF ELDERS

How does one measure the intentions of a life? What is an elder? What aligns our spirit to transcending purpose? What is the drive to self-transformation and assisting the transformations of others, in our families, in our communities, in our nations?

In Native traditional culture, *elder* denotes a person of special respect. The most highly considered elders carry a concentrated mindfulness about their own people. They carry a long-term sense of their societies and their generations. In their actions over time, they have evidenced great love for their peoples and communities.

Indigenous women have always held our communities together. We grow tall individually, but like elder trees in a forest, we maintain a deeply entwined thicket of roots under the surface. It is a world of our own, where we organize our offshoots and their seedlings, and visualize the future of our common children. It is from this vein that we wondered what could happen when Indigenous women elders intentionally align our spirits and together represent a connected circle. A whole movement of spiritually aligned Native women elders has grown from this question, and a first wave of legacy women, always the core of our Indigenous resilience, emerged.

Among various circles, we contemplated: What makes a Native woman an elder? We cast out in search of women who have led and sustained the best possibilities and potential for enhancing the cultural health and spiritual strength of their own generations. Many examples surfaced, as a wide array of such women exist in the Native world. Gradually, a first circle, a beginning, emerged.

People of transcending quality, the eight American Indigenous women elders whose oral narratives we are privileged to present, constitute a range of brilliant resistance and persistence of Native heritage—in cosmologies, philosophy, and depth of cultural practice. Each elder has been molded by her community and her passion, her vision. Two are Mohawk sisters from my own matrilineal roots; others are sister elders from across sacred landscapes of the Lakota, Cheyenne, Santa Clara Pueblo, Gwich'in, Chelalis, and Hopi peoples. They all present lives and narratives of challenge and courage, and profound lessons in womanhood and community. There is a teaching curriculum in their life stories, accumulated wisdom of a lived history that spans generations over three centuries. With each and all of them, we deepened the delightful process of getting to know of each other's lives and, I like to say, we began to line up our spirits.

Henrietta Mann shone through as elder of elders. Henrietta's narrative spans the generations, establishing a sense of where we come from, as women elders of Native communities. A trailblazer in the field of Native studies, and an early proponent of Indigenous-based education for American Indian students, Henrietta speaks about when her Cheyenne people had "nothing left but a will to survive and to encourage continuity."

Introduction

Henrietta is a distinguished intellectual; she is also lovingly respected as a Prayer Woman and Sun Dance leader—a formidable wisdom that straddles multiple generations. Into her nineties, Henrietta carries the essential continuity of intimate family oral memories of seemingly long-ago events, such as the horrific Sand Creek Massacre perpetrated in 1864. Her great-grandmother Vister was wounded during the massacre but escaped to survive. "My mother told how she was always fascinated by the deep wound that Vister carried in the back of her leg. As a little girl, she would often sit under the table and rub that bullet wound carried by her grandmother from the Sand Creek Massacre."

Henrietta's narrative and all of the elder stories carry lessons—approaches to life—that our young women activists might want to read and internalize. As we seek the ancient teachings in the path to our survival, we know that both challenges—the personal healing and the public struggle—are necessary for our communities. We grow, then we struggle. We struggle, then we grow.

There are many stories, just from the past few years. The intent is not necessarily to write them all down, but to share the significant threads in our collective memory. A powerful dream, for instance, led Loretta Afraid of Bear Cook, Oglala Lakota Elder, to reengage the rites of passage for young women of her reservation and their culture.

A longtime grassroots activist, Loretta's narrative gathers meaning from powerful lines of ancestor relatives that ushered her into consciousness. Loretta is one of those "chosen children" of earlier generations, when the older cousins were encouraged to spend much of their childhoods among the elders, to learn values, language, and skills experiencing life in the more ancient and traditional ways. Loretta's lifelong leadership in Sun Dance ceremonial cycles, and in mentorship among women, follow the teachings of her mother, renowned spiritual elder Beatrice Long Visitor Holy Dance, who for over fifty years fueled and guided many Lakota families (*tiospaye*) in the preservation of their traditional lifeways. Loretta reminds us, "The good things I was taught, they survive, and we are working hard to strengthen our people. But we are working inside a very harsh reality. Our history inside these United States has not been easy. We have been massacred by American troops, in our own homelands, and this history still surrounds us."

As in all the narratives, Loretta's range of ceremonial teachings with the younger women intricately binds to the sacred landscape of her ancient nation in the northern Great Plains, and the struggle for the preservation of spiritual and material authority over their sacred Black Hills, the Paha Sapa, "the heart of all there is."

We sometimes think of legacy in terms of wealth. But wisdom sees *relational* wealth, the one that flows from our interconnections within the web of life, as the most important wealth, if you can manage it.

Wakérakats:te Louise Herne, Mohawk Clan Mother, has emerged as a powerful voice for the strength and participation of women, both in the traditional Longhouses and in the world at large. Louise has forged wide networks of Native women leaders, inspiring and fostering their interconnections while strengthening their capacity for mindfulness through isolation, contemplation and fasting, and activism. Her narrative takes us through the making of a clan mother, and her own effort to revitalize the rites of passage ceremonies for young women and men. This work has spawned an important movement. Louise reminds us that it's "where the story begins to change. We are giving attention to the important points where monumental change needs to occur as our young people walk into adulthood."

"Becoming takes time," Nora Naranjo-Morse reminds us in her narrative. Nora is a Kha'p'o Tewa potter whose creative motion points out life's many power imbalances. As artist and cultural teacher in her community and nationally, she smooths these out in her daily work with clay and in her many activities with young people.

Nora focuses the many small articulations of culture, in the moments that pass between the generations, in the gestures of kindness and teaching among relatives. An elder keenly aware of the many relocations and disconnections brought by colonization, she sees the work of ceremony and of growing the traditional crops as "the gift of reconnecting to the Pueblo worldview."

"I am a modern-day elder," Nora tells us. "I approach and model cultural and community values as best as I can. I believe that our sense of culture can be articulated in many ways: ceremony, renewal of language, kindness. Those articulations of culture leave an imprint for new generations of Indigenous peoples."

Jan Kahehti:io Longboat is a beloved Mohawk leader from the Six Nations of the Grand River in Ontario. A renowned woman of knowledge, Jan is an elder's elder: a healer, a very respected herbalist, gardener, ceremonial leader, sought-after mentor, and advisor. She is a significant bridge person among the generations, at her home community and nationally.

Kahehti:io's significant contributions include her wise healing work with the generations of elders who underwent the miserable period of boarding schools. Under this arrogant national policy, and from which our families still suffer, Native children were forced to attend government and church boarding schools, away from family, in order to be intentionally alienated from their Native cultures. Jan carries forward a cohesive sense of Indigenous traditional life, as lived in her childhood. She refers to acts of "lateral kindness," in contrast to the "lateral violence" caused by the policies that Pope Francis of the Catholic Church has now defined as genocide. "We are in the throes of our healing time," Jan says. "The people are coming back to our foods, to appreciate our ways again. It makes me happy when our women come together and sing those seed songs and harvest songs. We're harvesting our food and saving our seeds again. It's important that the women lead."

Women learn from women and from men, yet carry forward and teach their knowledge as women. Sarah James, Gwich'in leader from Arctic Village in northern Alaska, is now internationally recognized for her advocacy on behalf of her people in their struggle against oil development of the Arctic National Wildlife Refuge, the breeding grounds for the caribou herds. "We have been a strong people, because we could live on the land," she says. "We are more settled now, but we still live with the land. I remember with my mom back when I was growing up out in the land. We had everything there. And today we've still got everything there."

Introduction

Sent out by her elder chiefs to represent their concern that oil development in their region would destroy their precious caribou herds, Sarah traveled and represented her tribe endlessly on the issue for over thirty years. She has been a successful advocate, whose teams of supporters have kept major corporations at bay for four decades. A quiet speaker, Sarah's quality is in the firmness of her message. "The Porcupine caribou herd is my life. It makes me who I am. My people grew up with caribou, depending on them for everything. In return, we also take care of the caribou and the environment so that our caribou are healthy. Our elders always say that we're in the caribou's heart and the caribou is in our heart, which means that they take care of us and, in return, we take care of them. We are proud of who we are, the caribou and us."

Being from a place and living in place, as Indigenous elders, we know how strongly we are formed by the natural world. We are embodied in those roots, which have been cut and scarred but have not been severed. Weaving is the way of embodiment for Yvonne Peterson, Toon Nee Mu Sh. A Chehalis elder dedicated to continuing in her people's traditional weaving, we hear in her words and see in her work the commitment to sustain in the pride of her mother's teachings and and continuous appreciation of her people's ecology.

"Weaving is a cultural knowledge," says Yvonne. "It links us to the past and will link us to the future. It is a connection to our history, our language."

Still attentive to our natural surroundings, belonging in a tapestry of relatives weaves us into the world, and makes us responsible for that world. "We have fought for our fishing rights as far as the United States Supreme Court. I see us moving forward within my lifetime to protect our plants, the way we eat them, use them for medicine and ceremonies, industry, and weaving." A professor at Evergreen College in Washington State, Yvonne knows that the roots of her educational work are in the consciousness of that relationship. "We begin with a prayer to recognize the teachings of the tree people. In our area, the trees are seen as the first teachers. For every tree, there's a teaching that they give to us."

Legacy is the path you leave behind. Living from your purpose, aligning with your spirit, the woman of legacy is grounded in deep interest and appreciation for the traditional knowledge of her ancestral homeland. Her community-based action is enlivened by her profound love of her people. She is gifted that knowledge and she must seek that knowledge, certain that it will help her make a life for herself and make a genuine contribution to her people.

A consciousness of helping her Hopi people envision and build their own future has driven the work of Barbara Poley and permeates her narrative. With presence of mind, and modest and perceptive silence based on traditional respect, her methodology of social change consistently elicits community people's own thinking and capacities as they face challenges and build on their own dreams.

"I think most of our people will recognize that what was done for and by Hopi, the survival of Hopi, the laws they developed for themselves, were based on simple things to keep people alive, keep people in good order. It's a system that was created as most community systems are created. The highest value is to take care of one another."

Fiercely independent and loyal to these highest values, Barbara's work modeled an everyday sovereignty. "People with funds who wanted to tell us what and how to do it, and said this is some money we have for you to do it this way, we immediately shut them off. We would not go further with them. No, they had to take us seriously about how much we knew about what our community needed."

Decades and decades of life cycles and sacrifice, achievements and disappointments, the love and pain and growth of families, clans, nations, the love of special places and doings, are all bundled in the experiences of these eight remarkable women elders. Intimations and orientations from eight long arcs of historical reality present us women who have lived and led their peoples to travel on healthier, more self-determined and self-actualizing roads. Their narratives provide a portrait of personal values and knowledge in social change. Woven from lives of valiant activism, they gift us a foundational post in the canon of nation-building and survival of Indigenous peoples.

By Katsi Cook

Akwesasne Mohawk (Wolf Clan)
Director, Spirit Aligned Leadership Program

"Our prayers are one long unbroken braid like sweetgrass."

DR. HENRIETTA MANN
Southern Cheyenne

D R. HENRIETTA MANN is a Cheyenne elder with direct ties to her people's ancient culture and with powerful memories of the historical forces that shaped today's Western plains. She grew up hearing stories of her valiant, resourceful women relatives and was resolute from an early age to educate herself and to teach her own people first. Enrolled in the Cheyenne-Arapaho Tribes of Oklahoma, Henrietta learned humility and compassion from her elders. She was identified in her infancy as a leader, and now enjoys life as a Sun Dance and ceremonial prayer woman.

As a child, Henrietta demanded to go to public school, where she endured racism and discrimination. She persevered to earn a PhD in American studies in 1982. Henrietta was a pioneer professor in setting the highest quality standards for the emergent field of Native American studies, which has since become an established academic discipline in the United States. She taught and mentored three generations of Native students in higher education, inspiring many to current positions of leadership throughout Indian country.

The founding president of the Cheyenne and Arapaho Tribal College, Henrietta was the first individual to occupy the endowed chair in Native American Studies at Montana State University–Bozeman, where she is professor emerita and served as special assistant to the president until 2016. She was among the main designers of the Native

American Studies programs at the University of California, Berkeley; the University of Montana; and Haskell Indian Nations University in Lawrence, Kansas.

Among her many honors, she received the Lifetime Achievement Award from the National Indian Education Association in 2008. Henrietta's book *Cheyenne-Arapaho Education: 1871-1982* is a classic in the field of American Indian education.

Prayer Cloth Woman

Peveešeeva. Good day to you.

My Cheyenne name is Ho'eoestaoonah'e, Prayer Cloth Woman, or the Woman Who Comes to Offer Prayer.

I was born in Oklahoma and am known to the Northern Cheyenne as having been born a "hair rope woman," meaning that our people continued to weave our ropes from buffalo hair. I lived and taught for some forty years with my Northern Cheyenne relatives, the Morningstar people of Montana.

My father was Horse Road and my mother was Day Woman. My grandfathers were Spotted Horse and Deer. Tragically, I never knew either one of my grandmothers, yet I am very blessed by having been named for my paternal grandmother, Ho'eoestaoonah'e—Prayer Cloth Woman. My maternal grandmother was Bertha Powder Face. I never knew her Cheyenne name. My great-grandmother's name was Vister.

The matriarch of our family was my paternal great-grandmother Vóestaā'e, or White Buffalo Woman. I would have loved to have lived the life she did, in terms of being free. She was born in the Territory of Wyoming around 1853, two years after the Cheyenne signed our 1851 Treaty of Fort Laramie.

The People to Whom I Belong

The people to whom I belong are Tsétsėhéstȧhese, the "people alike," known in English as Cheyenne.

Ma'heo'o created water, earth, sky, air, and sunlight before creating human beings. Ma'heo'o created beings to keep the Earth Grandmother company. In our story, the natural elements were too powerful to live together, so Ma'heo'o separated them. Man Person lives in the Southern Hemisphere, and brings the rain and thunder for spring and summer, and joins her for only a short time. Beautiful North Woman Person brings the cold and snow in fall and winter. She, too, leaves after a while. Then, the human beings were created.

After the people had lived for a time upon their Earth Grandmother, a prophet named Sweet Medicine came to them from their sacred teaching mountain, Bear Butte, near the Black Hills. He brought them all what makes them unique as Cheyenne. Another prophet, Erect Horns, brought to them the sacred Buffalo Hat and the Sun Dance, which is their female ceremony of renewal and ushers in the Cheyenne New Year.

The people alike have walked the Road of Life since creation. They have divided their history into the ancient time, the time of the dogs, the time of the buffalo, and the current period, the time of the horse. Over the time we have lived on earth we have maintained our teachings and ceremonial responsibilities to and for this beautiful Earth Grandmother.

Our Sacred Center

The Cheyenne have a special place that figures prominently in our cultural geography. Bear Butte is known to us as Noahà-vose, the hill that gives or teaches. It stands on the periphery of the Black Hills, and is the Cheyenne teaching mountain. Noahà-vose is considered a sacred site, where we go to pray, fast, seek direction for our hearts and minds, make offerings, say thank you. My grandfather always told me, "When you pray, you don't just ask. You've got to say thank you. Thank you for life. Thank you for breath. Thank you for sight. Thank you for being able to speak."

We pray to appreciate that we were given life specifically, according to our Cheyenne creation story, to keep this beautiful Earth Mother alive, to keep her company. We are to always be good stewards of the land, to protect Earth Mother, to love her, to walk on her in gentleness, because she supports our feet. She is very loving, kind, and continues to share with us the abundance that we need. In our view of the world, it's very important to be thankful, and to know that there is a sacred center to our universe.

Sweet Medicine received his teachings from within our sacred mountain, where all of the spirit powers of the world gathered to teach him the ways. There was the spirit of the buffalo, there was the spirit of the butterfly, there's the spirit of the bison, the spirit of the bear, the spirit of sage, the spirit of sweetgrass, the spirit of the sun, spirit of Grandmother Earth, or Mother Earth, spirit of Grandmother Moon, even the spirit of the rose. For four years they taught him these beautiful things that we are so fortunate to live with in this world. He brought all that was holy and good from out of that mountain, everything that is uniquely Cheyenne, our organization as a nation, specifically our Council of Peace Chiefs and Warrior Societies, our strong value systems, our lifeways. Sweet Medicine brought to us our spiritual way of life—how we are to be individually and collectively.

Bear Butte has stood her watch throughout time. Generations of Cheyenne and other peoples—Lakota, Dakota, Nakota, Arapaho, Kiowa, and others—still journey to this sacred place. I myself have fasted on the side of Bear Butte, and I have secured for myself a place on that sacred mountain forever. I have smoked a sacred pipe there several times, and have had the great honor of smoking the pipe with a Sacred Arrow Keeper at the mouth of Sweet Medicine Cave. I have participated in a sweat lodge there, and have tied prayer cloths to the trees that stand on the sides of Bear Butte. This place has strengthened my spirit many times. It is my spiritual home. I know that other Sun Dance women before me have gone there to pray, and I know that many generations of others will go there after me. Our prayers are one long unbroken braid like sweetgrass.

Bravehearts and Survivors

Both of my great-grandmothers were survivors of the Sand Creek Massacre of 1864 and the massacre along the Washita River in 1868.[1] If those two women had not had those brave hearts and not survived, I would not be here. My great-grandmother Vister was wounded at Sand Creek. The story is that her uncle threw her up on a pony, then hit it on its flanks so she could flee. The people said she rode the pony away, but remembered her little brother before she got too far. She turned that pony around and, with bullets whizzing around her, found her brother, pulled him up behind her, and fled to safety. She took a bullet to the back of her calf. They got away.

My mother said she was always fascinated by the deep wound that Vister carried in the back of her leg. As a little girl, she would often sit under the table and rub that bullet wound carried by her grandmother from the Sand Creek Massacre.

My elders did not talk about the massacres, as they were trying to coexist with the new settlers and were afraid of being incarcerated. My mother always told me that the people had been very happy at Sand Creek. They thought they were in a place of safety and peace and played social games way into the night, little suspecting that the Methodist minister John Chivington was bringing his troop of 700 men to surprise them in a dawn attack.

---

1 The Washita River was known as the Lodge Pole River by the Cheyenne, who would lean their tepee poles against tall trees alongside the river when they broke camp for summer.

Warned that soldiers were approaching, Black Kettle, hailed as the most peaceable of all Cheyenne chiefs, gathered his children and people around him. Their camp flew the flag of the United States of America and a white flag of peace. Both had been quickly hoisted on a very tall lodge pole. He gathered them around those flags, believing, as he had been told, that no soldier would ever fire upon the US flag. They fired anyway. The attack resulted in the deaths of hundreds of Cheyenne, most of them women and children.

Three investigations, two congressional and one military, found that the savagery of that massacre belies even the human imagination. Soldiers cut fetuses from the wombs of their mothers, and made saddle horn covers and hat bands from male and female genitalia. The scalps of our people were paraded into what was then Denver City and put on display at the Apollo Hall. The Sand Creek Massacre has been decried as the most savage killing of Indigenous people of this land.

I often think of that massacre and recall the bravery and the courage of our grandparents, only three generations removed from me, who endured attacks by the United States military. To have survived at all speaks to the bravehearted women and men, and the children who grew up and gave life to us so that we survive and still carry that courage, that bravery. I also carry the blood memory of the savagery and inhumanity of people that valued property over people, that valued their own prosperity over human lives.

"I carry the blood memory of the savagery and inhumanity of people that valued property over people."

GROWING UP AS AN ONLY CHILD

We still have our territory as Cheyenne and Arapaho. It's a checkerboard pattern of tribal lands over nine counties in western Oklahoma. After Black Kettle and his wife were killed at the lodge pole, one of the chiefs became a leader of Whiteshield. He established an Indian camp and concentrated people from this band around him. I can remember growing up, wanting to live in Whiteshield camp. They lived in canvas army tents, with dirt floors sometimes covered in cardboard or tar paper to keep in warmth. There was always a cast-iron stove in the one-room lodge. It was always a happy place. They had a community bond that I have never seen anymore.

We did not live in Whiteshield camp. I grew up on my grandfather's allotment in the western portion of our territory, in Hammon, Oklahoma. By not living in the camp, we were sort of once-removed. We lived in a little community called McClure, six or seven miles northeast of Hammon. We weren't the only family that lived on their Indian allotment, on a farm family allotment. For those of us who did not live in the camp, there was some friction. Sometimes people can be so cruel. We would be told, "What do you want, to live like a White man?" and "You don't even speak your language." Not to me, though, because I did speak my language. My family made sure that I learned as much as I could. I was culturally steeped.

My father, Horse Road Henry Mann, and my grandfather, Spotted Horse Fred Mann, were members of the Peyote Church. I grew up in the Peyote Way. I was bonded to those two men. When they were going to go off to a peyote meeting, I would go, too. I would get all dressed up. My mother would braid my thick hair tightly. There I'd go walking down the railroad track or down the road with my father and grandfather to those Saturday night peyote meetings. One would carry a little blanket and the other a little pillow. There was always extra for me, and I'd sit there. Toward morning, after the midnight smoke and I began to get sleepy, one would take that blanket and make my little bed back behind them and say, "Okay, now you go to sleep for a little bit."

I grew up alone. I was virtually an only child. I did not have any siblings until I was nearly twelve. As a child I pestered my parents, "I want a little brother. I want a little sister." They would say, "You've got your cousins." Yes, they're my brothers and sisters, too, but I wanted my own.

While I was working on a doctorate degree in the 1980s my dad said, "Sister, come here. I guess I can tell you this now so you understand." He said, "When you were going to be born, your mother and I made the decision that we would have no other children for ten years." That was one of our Cheyenne customs. Sometimes parents would take an oath specifying a period of time when they would have no more children. Mine wanted to make sure that I had all of the training, knowledge, love, teachings, whatever I needed. I was very blessed to discover that my parents took that vow to make sure I got the best that was possible in the 1930s and '40s.

My dad was my best friend. He went off to World War II as I was entering junior high. He was wounded in Germany and awarded a Purple Heart. When he left to the army we had to give up farming, which was a Bureau of Indian Affairs (BIA) program. We moved to Clinton, Oklahoma, where I had been born, before my dad left for the service. He was a very good man when he left. He came back an alcoholic.

Years later, I interviewed him while I was working on my doctorate degree. "Sister," he said, "I never want you to experience war. War is the most horrible thing that I can think of." He wondered about the things that his grandmother must have gone through at Sand Creek. He told me, "Every day before we'd go out to battle, they would give us a choice of whiskey or whatever. We'd take it and then we'd go out to battle. I got hooked on it."

My father wasn't the same when he returned from war. He became a wanderer. He called it his twenty-five-year walk in a fog. Then, for the last dozen years of his life, he was sober. My father had finally come home from the war, the father that I knew.

My mother was a very good student, a product of the Indian Affairs boarding schools. She was a perfect housekeeper, a phenomenal cook, and could sew clothing. She was a very good Mennonite Christian woman. I went to Sunday school with her; she was a teacher. Toward the middle of her life, she and my father went out to Los Angeles as part of the BIA's Indian relocation program.[2] She became an evangelist in the Foursquare Gospel Church. In the summertime, we participated in our tribal ceremonies.

Beloved Grandma

I learned what true love and friendship are from Vóestaá'e, White Buffalo Woman. Very fortunately, we spent four wonderful years together. "Your feet never touched the ground," my father told me. "She was old but still managed to hold you constantly," he said. "You and my grandmother—your great-grandmother—had a very loving relationship."

---

2 The Indian Relocation Act of 1956 was a US law intended to encourage American Indians to leave Indian reservations and their traditional lands, and to assimilate into the general population in urban areas.

"*Vóestaā'e introduced me to the spirit powers of the world with a baby pipe ceremony.*"

Henrietta in 1978

She was my first teacher. I remember jumping out of a slowly moving car to many shouts of "Stop!" as I flung open the door and hit the ground running. I could not get to grandma's house fast enough. I crawled up the steps and ran into the open arms of the only grandmother I ever knew, who sat waiting for me with a smile. I can say emphatically that this woman, the last of the Southern Cheyenne buffalo and horse people, was my beloved and my first great love. When I came to walk on this earth, she told my dad, "You know, this is an answer to my daily prayers. I prayed every day to live long enough to see your child." And that child is me.

Vóestaā'e introduced me to the spirit powers of the world with a baby pipe ceremony. These great powers sit in the four sacred directions of the universe and watch over all human beings. In the four brief years our lives overlapped she managed to teach me what it is to be one of the people, and I absorbed from her what it is to live a life of service. What she could not teach me, she left to her son and grandson to teach me. When they would say to me, "My mother said," or "My grandma said," I knew my grandma Vóestaā'e was talking to me.

Most of those who have served as my mentors have walked up the great, wide road of the Milky Way in the sky to live in that gigantic encampment in the stars.

A Determined Student

As a child, I liked to learn. Storytelling was a good time for me. A cousin who had come to live with us would come home from Hammon School and we would play school. She'd say, "Today I learned the vowels. Let's go in and learn the vowels." She would pretend to be the teacher. Playing school, I learned the vowels *a, e, i, o, u*. My dad saw what was going on, so he went out and got an old piece of a blackboard from the abandoned boarding school that was just about a half mile down the road from where we lived.

He mounted it in my mother's little pantry and set up some desks. There was a shelf for all my books. Of course he got permission from Mr. Rennick, the Indian agent. It's tragic how these agents could control our lives, even at that point in time. So my father made a little schoolroom in that area, complete with the blackboard and erasers that came from a school that had been abandoned for a very long period of time. I was taught by my older cousins who are essentially my sisters, and I learned much. I learned to count to one hundred, I learned my colors, I learned all the vowels. I was rather advanced. I really loved this kind of education. Even as a child, I knew what I wanted and how to go about getting it.

One day my mother told my dad, "This child is driving me crazy. She wants to go to school and she's not of the age yet." I had just turned five. One night over dinner, my dad said, "Sister, your mom told me you want to go to school." And I said, "Yes, yes!"

He said, "You can go to school with Joyce when she comes home." I said, "No, I want to go to the real school. I want to ride that big yellow bus!" He promised they'd think about it. One day, my mother told me Mr. Rennick was coming into town soon. "And Mr. Jones, the education agent," added my dad. "We have to talk to Mr. Rennick. So get ready."

I don't know if I slept that night. I got up early and we went down to the abandoned school, which is where the Indian agent's office was when he came to town. There, Mr. Rennick walked around and inspected me like you would an animal. I would ordinarily ask, "What are you doing?" But my mother stood there, signaling me to be quiet.

"Well, she looks okay," he said. He asked me some questions and I answered them. Finally, he said, "Okay, you can send her to school." Oh my gosh! Music to my ears. I could go to school! Then I heard him say, "Go ahead and send her to school. She's so young that when she gets tired of the tempo, you can pull her back out."

So off to school I went. My grandfather would walk about a mile down the railroad tracks to put me on the yellow school bus. I loved it.

My grandfather told me, "We sent your dad to Concho because at that point not all of us got an education, but we wanted some of our young people to go to those schools so that they could be those bridges between cultures." We weren't going to send all of our children to those schools, but we sent some so they could be bridges from our cultures, as Cheyenne, out to the world. I found out some went to Chilocco Indian School, Haskell Indian Industrial School, Genoa Indian School, and Carlisle Indian School in Pennsylvania. Here on our reservation, it was the Concho Indian School. They looked upon their students as interpreters of culture, the bridges between two separate ways of life.

Heartbreak and a Life-Changing Decision

I went off to Hammon public school. I liked it, but there I learned that it was different for Indians. The Indian children were all placed in the back of the room. None of us could sit in the front with the non-Indian children. And not once were we called on to answer any questions. The teachers would often ask these little non-Indian children to go out and dust the erasers, and they'd go out and play and clap the erasers. No Cheyenne child, from the camp or the allotments, was ever asked to dust those erasers. We were tolerated but basically ignored.

One day, when I was in third or fourth grade, the little Cheyenne children began to disappear out the door. I wondered what was going on. Finally, they took me out into the hallway and there was the school nurse along with some mothers of the non-Indian children and some people from the church all standing in the hall, inspecting the Indian children for head lice.

That was really humiliating. None of the non-Indian children were asked to get their heads examined, just us. Some had lice and some didn't. That day, I didn't. I would, sometimes, go and visit in the camps. My mother and aunt would know when I came home to check my head. Sometimes I got lice, sometimes I didn't. That day I had no lice, and I was allowed to go back into the classroom.

School was out and I got on the bus. It was no longer this big beautiful yellow bus because once we got going, the other students began chanting, "Dirty Indian! Lousy Indian!" I rode the bus for three miles to those taunts. I just sat there. This is so unfair, I thought. I know that some of us are cleaner than some of our non-Indian classmates. I saw the mothers go down to the Washita River and wash their children's clothing to make sure they were clean when they went to school.

I guess that's where I learned what you might call stoicism. Being quiet helped me on that bus ride. I got off the bus and looked down the railroad tracks. I could see my grandfather coming down to meet me and I started crying as I ran to him. He hurried to me and threw his arms around me and just held me. I was brokenhearted that day. That was my first experience with discrimination, how mean and cruel it was to single out us Cheyenne.

"Let us walk home," my grandfather said, "Just calm down and when we get home, we'll talk." He only spoke Cheyenne, never English. He's one who showed up at the gates of Chilocco Indian

School and declared, "I'm coming to school but I'll only be here as long as I want." He stayed for one year. I didn't even know if he could speak English, although I thought he had to know because he would read a newspaper and when televisions came he would watch baseball games.

We got home. After I'd changed clothes, I told him what happened at school. I was still having the aftereffects of the tears. "I'm not going back to school," I cried. "Mr. Rennick said that my mom and dad could pull me out if I no longer wanted to go and I'm going to tell them this evening that they can pull me out of school right now."

"Well, you can tell them that," he said, "but I don't know that it's going to happen. You're too far along."

"Why did they treat us like this?" I pleaded. "Why didn't the teacher say something?" I had so many questions. He said, "Maybe one of these days, you want to become a teacher. Maybe you want to be like those teachers in the classroom that will treat all of you Indian children well."

I decided then, at about eight years of age, that I was going to become a schoolteacher so that the Indian children like me would not get treated in the way that was customary in the school system, with discrimination and lack of respect. I would teach no one but Indian children. I still had trouble with English, but I was going to teach them how to speak English because that was something that I really lacked. I was going to teach them about how we live, how we are, and that we're human beings, too. That was always my goal.

A Commitment to Indian Education

I graduated from high school in 1951, then went on to Southwestern State College on a scholarship from a teacher's organization. I majored in English education. After I graduated from Oklahoma State University in 1970 with my master of arts degree in English, a new discipline was brought to my attention: Native American studies. I contacted San Francisco State University for a job. A man answered the phone. He kindly introduced himself as Richard Oakes, a Mohawk, and mentioned he had been out for a time and just happened to be in the office that day.[3] Curious, I asked where he had been.

"We're out on the Rock," he said. "Alcatraz."

They were not hiring, he told me, and recommended I call UC Berkeley, which was looking for someone for its Native American studies program.

"If we were hiring, I would have hired you," Richard said, "But you'd have to come out to the Rock."

With the desire to teach no one but Indian children, I called UC Berkeley. In March 1970 I went off to teach Native American studies and found my place in education. It was disheartening, though, when I went to my first university class to find that I didn't have any Indian students. They were still out on the Rock. I have always been an activist in my own way, and teaching at UC Berkeley provided me the

---

3 Richard Oakes (May 22, 1942 – September 20, 1972) was a Mohawk activist who helped spur Native American studies in university curricula before becoming a leader of the occupation of Alcatraz. Oakes is credited for helping to change US policy from termination to self-determination.

forum to articulate the injustice of American Indian life. I supported the movement because some of my students were very active in the Alcatraz occupation. We each have our own style in achieving the purpose for which we were put on earth.

At that time, Native American studies was so new that we were part of ethnic studies, which included Asian, Black, and Chicano studies. We would all go into sessions as coordinators and the Black faculty would say, "We're going to make a final decision because we've come to be the largest minority population in the country," and then the Chicanos would say, "Oh, no, you're not. We constitute the largest population in the Southwest." Then the Asians would say, "Don't go there. We constitute the largest minority population in the Bay Area." Then I'd say, "Well, it's not really quantity that counts. It's quality. We were here first and our teachings derive from this land and so I will make the final decision."

They would call me their diplomat. I don't know that I'm so diplomatic now, but there was a time when I was. It was difficult because, as an academic discipline, there were many of those in the academy that looked down upon cultural studies.

I stayed at Berkeley for almost three years. It was rewarding, but the big city was too much for me. I was offered a position in Washington state but I chose the University of Montana because it was near the Northern Cheyenne reservation.

I taught at UM for twenty-eight years and advanced through the ranks to become a full professor. I left because I was offered an endowed chair position at Montana State University,[4] one of only a handful of such positions in Native American studies programs in the country at that time.

I just loved my classes with the Indian students. I did a lot of individual and collective mentoring. It was my time to give back, to help them cultivate the skills and knowledge they needed to graduate and go out and work in this world. Just like my grandparents before me, I looked upon education as a way for our students to gain a very strong sense of identity and knowledge of their culture as well as what is taught in the usual academic classroom.

I would have special evening sessions with them on their writing. When I was interviewed in 1991 about being named by *Rolling Stone* magazine as one of the ten leading professors in the nation, I learned that my students referred to me as Dragon Lady. I was so upset by that! My interviewer said, "No, no, no. They mean it in a good way. They said they used to just be horrified about getting their papers back from you because they would be so marked up in red."

I retired from MSU in 2003. It was a challenge to work in Native American studies because of some of those in the ivory tower, so to speak, didn't want us to be on campus at all. Each one of us is born with a purpose and I thought, alright, I have probably achieved my purpose. I like to think that I helped to establish and legitimize Native American studies throughout the country. I hope that our Indian educators and researchers today have much less to be concerned about in terms of attitudes of other professors on their campuses.

---

4 Henrietta was the first to occupy the endowed chair in Native American Studies at Montana State University.

I believe in education. My time in the classroom was devoted to building cross-generational bridges and teaching about our cultures to the succeeding generations, which was my dream job. Many of my contemporaries thought it was nothing more than working as a slave in the trenches of Indian education. But education is much more than that.

Our ancestors knew that we had to be educated in our ways, but that we also had to learn these new ways, these different ways brought to us by these strangers who came to live with us. We had to learn to speak their language, which is why I majored in English—to develop those speaking and writing skills. Education, in that regard, is necessary. Native American Studies is critical in helping our young people graduate from college and university. We have learned about our history as a people and about the injustice that we suffered in the American Indian wars and in the movements to achieve our place or to maintain our place in society.

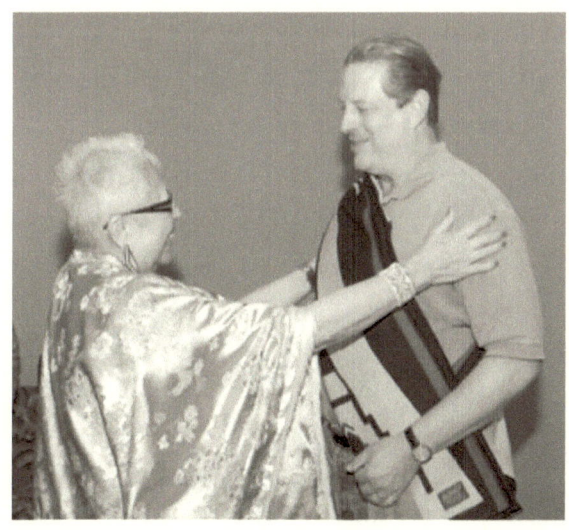

Henrietta and Al Gore, National Museum of the American Indian, 2007

Henrietta awarded National Humanities Medal from President Joe Biden, 2023

My leadership role in Indian education has definitely been sustained by the love I have for both Native American studies and for the students, as well as for their potential. I am happiest that many students still carry the strong sense of identity and history with them that they developed in those places of higher learning. I like to think that Native American Studies programs and departments have helped contribute to their success in the Indian and the non-Indian world. They have not disappointed me, for some of them are now university professors, medical doctors, doctors of philosophy/education, attorneys, tribal college presidents, teachers, and so on. Every day in my prayers and when I sit in ceremony, I thank Ma'heo'o for sustaining me throughout the years and blessing me with such good students and my dream career.

Spirituality as a Teaching Art

I completed my PhD in American studies in 1982, and in 1988 I began my life as a Sun Dance ceremonial prayer woman. Both dramatically expanded my ways of knowing and ways of being, and each carries with it a joyful but forever responsibility.

As much as I love those whom I teach in a formal classroom situation or informally in the community, what I love to impart to them are our cultural ways as the first peoples of our beautiful motherlands. The wisdom of our grandparents is second to none when we understand that we live in an interdependent, interrelated universe made up of the basic elements of life—earth, air, fire, and water—and that for many peoples all life is contained within the sacred circle of life.

About twenty years ago, we brought this concept down from a college level course to a younger girls' project on one of Montana's seven Indian reservations. We called it the Seven Cheyenne Stars and Hope. I was the elder teacher, and the girls worked with professional mentors of their choice. We learned their reservation's history, visited important historical sites, made a pilgrimage to their sacred site, studied their tribal language, and had leadership development workshops, and I taught them about our concept of interdependence and value systems.

We had great fun over that two-year period. The girls were particularly pleased by the inclusiveness that was incorporated in the learning circle. It was a dramatic change, to go from teaching college students to working with younger women. They were at a teachable moment in their lives, which is different from working in a mixed community setting. There, elders are expected to be patient. But this is not true always for a university professor, so

I had to learn to balance the scale. Respect is necessary in good community relationships, and that applies in the classroom. What worked best for me with college students, with youth, and in the community is a combination of patience and respect.

My Giveaway Ceremony is Teaching

I was professor emerita at Montana State University–Bozeman when I took the challenge to engage in an encore career as president of Cheyenne and Arapaho Tribal College in my western Oklahoma backyard. I learned a lot about our communities and who we were as a people during those eight years. My purpose is to give away my education, to educate our youth in such a way that it reinforces their identities and makes them proud of who they are as this country's first children. My giveaway is premised on the fact that I have always believed in the value of an education, which is the reason I invested in getting the best one I possibly could.

In my trips throughout Cheyenne and Arapaho territory, I could not help but be appalled by the lack of educational opportunity and seeing our precious children still living with the same racism I endured. Regardless, I just love them all and want to tell them their world will be better. How can I make it better for them, except to help them strengthen their cultural ways of knowing and being?

Resilience to Carry On

Vóestaā'e lived to be eighty-five. I'm two years older, in terms of longevity. When she introduced me to the spirit powers of the world, my dad never told me what her prayer was. But I think I know. At that time it was the belief of the Cheyenne people that we needed interpreters, bridges between Indigenous and non-Indian cultures. Those bridges were not for everybody to build. Only a select few were going to be essentially given up to learn and bring those teachings back to those who stayed in their lodges, immersed in their ways.

Maybe it was nothing else but a will to survive and encourage continuity. We are very adaptable. We respect change in our lives. We're resilient. Our lifeways are resilient. Our grandparents respected change. They knew that change is the only thing about life that continues.

I was very blessed that my parents took that vow to not have another child for ten years, to make sure that I got the best that was possible in the 1930s and '40s. I didn't have a sibling until I was twelve. I had such great love for my brother, Henry. We called him Butch. He would call me Sister-Mama. Unfortunately, he passed away from alcoholism the first year I went to work on my doctorate degree. So I had to deal with the loss of my only sibling.

The morning I got the call that I passed my comprehensives, it was such a joyous day. We were at lunch at the Indian Pueblo Cultural Center, and my husband, who had been doing dialysis at home three times a week even while I was in grad school, started to feel chest pain. He wanted to get on dialysis so we took him home. We were getting ready to put him on the machine and he collapsed on our bed. We called an ambulance and within an hour he was gone. Again, I had a decision to make whether to continue.

I lost my brother, then my husband. It was a critical decision. What should I do? Give up my doctorate degree? I have a responsibility to my children now. I no longer had a husband. So I made the decision to continue in school. In 1982, without him, I got my PhD in American studies from the University of New Mexico.

"I thank Ma'heo'o for sustaining me throughout the years, and blessing me with such good students and my dream career."

Henrietta named National American Indian Woman of the Year 1987

So what do you do about that? You just do. You don't have anyone whispering in your ear, but you know that decisions come from the heart or out of a sense of unconditional love. I continued on with my doctorate work because I knew it was something my great-grandmother and my late husband both wanted. It was something that we as Indigenous peoples needed, to have those same credentials and to be acknowledged as having a voice—the right kind of voice.

My parents and grandparents prepared me to live a life of service, and to try to live as good a life a person can live despite all the challenges we face, like the loss of two important men in my life in the midst of trying to get a doctorate degree. Maybe sometimes the goal and the burden of responsibility had to be there. Can I do this? Will I be able to? After wanting a sibling for so long, can I go on and live without him? I know my husband wanted me to get that doctorate degree. I looked at my children and I thought, I've got sole responsibility.

Henrietta and Oprah Winfrey at Smith College, Northhampton, MA, as they both receive Honorary Doctorates, 2017

I don't know that I've ever had the luxury of deciding that I was not going to do something. One just does, despite the obstacles that we or our young women confront in a challenging time because of who we are as this land's first people. We just do. I certainly can understand the challenges because I've had more than my share.

A Peaceful Revolutionary

It wasn't an easy thing for me to go up the academic ladder as an Indian woman, to be promoted from assistant to associate professor and to finally make full professor at the University of Montana.

I could have stopped there. Then I was asked to fill the first endowed chair in Native American studies at MSU. I said, why not? You just do. Some of my colleagues at UM thought I had taken leave of my senses to leave an institution where I had gained tenure as a full professor. It was time for me to coast until retirement. Instead, I became an endowed chair, which was sort of icing on the cake.

After I retired in 2003 I became special assistant to two presidents. I stayed in the world of academia because it was my way of helping to educate our younger people. I once gave an interview to OSU where I got my master's. The article was titled "A Peaceful Revolutionary," which is the way I saw myself. Can a revolutionary be peaceful? Can a peaceful person be revolutionary? I felt that was what I was doing in the classroom for the non-Indian students, giving them a glimpse into a world that had much more balance and harmony, love, and respect for all life and all peoples. Again, it was just something that an individual like me had to do.

I cannot help but think those were the visions of my great-grandmother Vóestaá'e. I hope when it's my time to meet her again, I can look her in the face and say I did my best—which is all we can do. All we do is be the best that we can possibly be, nothing more than that. Be the best of who you are, who you can be. Always appreciate that most precious gift of love, precious gift of life. For as Cheyenne we journey around this earth one time and we'd better be the best we can possibly be in terms of kindness, love, cooperation, courage, compassion, patience, bravery. That's who a good Cheyenne and Indigenous woman is. We carry all of those positive characteristics to be a woman of strength and honor, to be bravehearted.

People like me are not going to be around forever, and there comes a time when that responsibility for the continuity of our lives, culture, languages, customs, and traditions must be transferred. I am very impressed with what Mama Bear does with the young people to maintain those very necessary aspects of ceremony, to make sure those times in one's life are acknowledged.[5] There's an accountability to the past and to the future, to our children. It just has to be. I just do the best I can to make life better for those generations that walk after me and carry it in such a way that it honors our beloved ancestors.

"I hope when it's my time to meet my great-grandmother Vóestaā'e again, I can look her in the face and say I did my best."

---

5 Mama Bear is an affectionate name for Louise Herne, Bear Clan Mother of the Mohawk Nation and fellow Legacy Leader.

"My duty is to make sure that my children and my grandchildren are going to know where they come from and how they came to be there."

Loretta Afraid of Bear Cook
Oglala Lakota

LORETTA AFRAID OF BEAR COOK is among the gems of the Indigenous traditional world. She is a natural inheritor of her Lakota people's extensive knowledge and a fluent speaker of their ancient language. Loretta is individually endowed with extraordinary memory, curiosity, and intelligence, a noble woman elder bundled in the high character and guidance of master teachers.

Her community and cultural world is an important core foundation of the extensive traditional world of the Lakota-Nakota-Dakota kinship that extends throughout the Great Plains of the United States and Canada. Loretta is at the forefront of contemporary movement on the central cultural issue of her people: the resolution of use and ownership of Paha Sapa, the sacred Black Hills. She possesses mastery over all of the ceremonial rituality associated with the tradition of the Sacred Pipe, Sun Dance, and other spiritual practices that promote unity.

Loretta's vision recognizes Native relatives and all people of good will, wherever they are situated, and moves us toward restoration of spirit and sacred space.

In 2018, Loretta received an honorary doctorate degree from the University of Alaska–Fairbanks.

Sharing Our Ways

I share this much of our ways because the word needs to get out just how important our family traditions are and, on a greater level, how important our nation's traditions are. Mostly, these are the teachings of my Afraid of Bear and my American Horse families—what I learned growing up, and how they imparted that knowledge to me.

Očhéthi Šakówiŋ

I come from Očhéthi Šakówiŋ, or the Seven Council Fires of the Lakota. I'm Oglala, part of what is called by others the Great Sioux Nation. I am Tetowan Oglala, from the western part of our ancestral homelands in what is known today as South Dakota.

I am from Pine Ridge, the largest of nine reservations in South Dakota. Each reservation has its own tribal government, but prior to that we each had very strong leadership within each band, which is akin to a very large extended family. We had strong and dedicated men leaders and we had women leaders of great fortitude and wisdom.

"Our heart and our future is bound in the Black Hills."

Our *tiospaye* follows the seven sacred ceremonies of Očhéthi Šakówiŋ, brought to us by the creator known as Skan, the great movement or great vibration, and Wo'ope, "Mother Law," our most beautiful feminine. Our ceremonies govern all aspects of Lakota life. From the Očhéthi Šakówiŋ, we have many relatives. I suspect that if we trace our lineages, each person with the Lakota, Nakota, and Dakota nations shares blood from each of those seven fireplaces.

The Slim Buttes community, where I was born, is not far from our sacred Black Hills, Paha Sapa. For Lakota, and for all Native peoples from the Plains, the Black Hills are the center of all that there is. The most sacred altars and prayer places are in the Black Hills. Our heart and our future is bound in the Black Hills.

Our Creation Story

We're an oral people, so that means our storytellers are our historians. They tell us that the Great Sioux Nation came from the stars, from a planet beyond the Pleiades. We originally came to the Earth Mother in a very soft vessel while it was still being formed and sank down into the mud. We lived beneath the earth in the Black Hills, until conditions on the surface were ready for us to emerge from what we call the Wind Cave.

These stories also say that we came from the stars. The constellation known as the Pleiades—or the Seven Sisters in our tradition—is part of the star map to our original home. The Seven Sisters have a butte in the Black Hills named after them because they were the maidens who went up into the sky to hold those places. The Seven

Sisters remind us that we come from somewhere, and we're going somewhere.

When we sit in our tepees and look up through the hole in the middle of the tepee where the poles come together, we recognize that as the portal to the next dimension. That is how we get from here to the Sky World. These flesh and blood bodies are the gift we get to enjoy for as long as we're on earth. They're on loan to us from every facet of life—from the air, the waters, the earth, the plants, the other animals, the sun, and even from Grandmother Moon. All these elements conspire to give us life. We are thankful to have it so we need to take good care of it. We're given life so that we can enjoy the gift, and then we give it back to the earth.

Tiospaye

I was born at home in November 1947 to Beatrice Long Visitor Holy Dance and Ernest Afraid of Bear. The midwife in attendance was one of my grandmothers, who was brought by wagon five or six miles in the snow to deliver me. Jenny Iron Rope was the first midwife that I am aware of from our Slim Buttes community. Grandma Jenny's husband was another medicine man, John Iron Rope. John did all the healing and all of the traditional ceremonies for the people there.

My grandfather was Brave Bear. He was father of Afraid of Bear, who had a brother named George Sword, or Mato Kagisni Iyanke in Lakota. A holy man, he advised us that anyone may learn the seven sacred rites. "These ceremonies are for us to give, not for us to keep," he said. My grandmother Antonia Sierra, a medicine woman, passed two years before I was born.

As the first grandchild of both my mother's and father's families, I got to attend ceremonies with my maternal grandfather, Rex Long Visitor Holy Dance. I was always by his side as a young child, safe to learn the inner workings of the Lakota way of being. It is in this beautiful manner that knowledge was transferred from elders to youth. In this way, I was able to make my own decision and commitment to humbly carry forward, to the best of my ability, the work of many of my ancestors.

Even as a child, I loved going to ceremony. My grandparents were there and all the elements, too—the fire, the wind. When I heard the rattles and drums begin, and the beating wings of eagles, and the little voices begin to speak…all the spiritual experiences that were very strong in my people, I loved every bit. I kept it inside. I would give it to anybody who wanted it. I would invite my friends to come with me to ceremony.

I learned our songs and prayers and found out about the people's hopes and determination to preserve our Očhéthi Šakówiŋ way of life. I am the oldest cousin. I have very many cousins who are like brothers and sisters. Being the oldest, they always looked up to me for direction. So I would try to impart what I know about the teachings of the uncles and the aunties. I was brought up in a really traditional manner. That is to say, I was told very early that these are your fathers, and these are your mothers. All of my mother's sisters are my mothers. All of my father's sisters are my teaching and teasing aunts.

My mother gave me life and prepared me well for the spirit journey that I have followed all of my seventy-three years. She taught me about the seven sacred rites and laws of Očhéthi Šakówiŋ: Purification Ceremony, Sun Dance, Vision Quest, Making of Relatives, Girl's Coming of Age, Tossing the Ball, and Keeping of the Spirit. As a young person under the wing of my relatives, I was blessed that my mother prepared me to carry out all seven rites.

My Afraid of Bear-Sword and Long Visitor Holy Dance families had the courage to pass onto their grandchildren the Oglala language, ceremonial ways, and knowledge of sacred sites. They are the foundation of my Oglala Lakota way of being.

Stronghold of Ancestral Knowledge

At the turn of the twentieth century, the Oglala Sioux had four remaining community "Shirt Wearers," who were the standard-bearers for the Oglala people. They made sure the people under their protection had food and shelter. They looked out for the old and infirm, the widows and orphans. My uncle Joe American Horse said there were community people that were selected in each of the tiospaye or kinship bands. They were put there to take care of the people, to protect and to serve.

That Shirt Wearer tradition is internal in my family. My grandfather George Sword was one of them. The other three Shirt Wearer men were Young Man Afraid of His Horses, American Horse, and Crazy Horse.

Sometimes, in museums, one can find buckskin shirts decorated with beads or porcupine quills, with hair all down the sleeves on both sides. Some people called them hair shirts, and that's how we say it, but they were actually community shirts. The communities put these shirts on the men they trusted, those who would take care of everybody—and the hair that was sewn into the sleeves was hair the people pulled from the crowns of their own heads. The crown—the fontanel in a newborn—we consider the most sacred part of the human body. Hair, generally, we consider sacred.

In 1887 the Dawes General Allotment Act resulted in sale of our lands to incoming settlers.[1] For decades, the settler government made many attempts to form a new Indian leadership. The federal government and the churches worked to put aside or destroy our natural, traditional tribal leaders. That eventually culminated in the 1934 Indian Reorganization Act government.[2] Before that, it was the Old People, the Big Bellies, the Silent Eaters, the Shirt Wearers, who told the people what was going to happen—for instance, that we were going to be put on reservations. I'm pretty sure there was a lot of sadness and anger because they were being displaced, but at the same time, the community was together.

---

1 The General Allotment Act or Dawes Act (1887) provided incoming White settlers free or very cheap Indian tribal and treaty lands. Ninety million acres passed from Indian to White "ownership." Remaining Indian land underwent substantial fragmentation. It was through the allotment process that Plains reservations became "checkerboarded" in complex patterns of white-owned private property and Indian trust lands.

2 The Indian Reorganization Act (IRA) or the Wheeler–Howard Act (1934) was US federal legislation intended to strengthen elective tribal government and halt the policy of eliminating the reservation bases. It did so for many tribal nations. A negative effect was to diminish the role of traditional and elder authorities among Native nations. It was the main legislation of what has been often called the "Indian New Deal."

As we transitioned to a life within the new reservation system, a lot of our practices were lost or at least put deeply away. We couldn't maintain them anymore—following the buffalo, for example, which was central to our culture and our main economic base. The naming of community Shirt Wearers was lost, too, because the men couldn't take responsibility for all their people, and sometimes they were persecuted as traditional chiefs. But we made an effort to preserve what was essential to our way of life by always imbuing some of our people with language, tradition, and ceremony.

The honor to protect and to serve has always been in my family. My duty is to make sure that my children and my grandchildren are going to know where they come from and how they came to be there.

Family Ways Shattered

The good things I was taught, they survive, and we are working hard to strengthen our people. But we are working inside a very harsh reality. Our history inside these United States has not been easy. We have been massacred by American troops, in our own homelands, and this history still surrounds us.

The United States attempted to take away all of the things I'm telling you about now, everything that was ours. Its laws and policies were meant to force us to abandon our deepest cultural ways. Whole families stopped speaking their language, their children were taken away and forced into boarding schools.

We call our children sacred little beings, up to the age of eleven years or so. We implore the Creator to let us keep them, not to take them back. We make sure to pay attention to them and give them love and honor. We make time for them even if we are doing something else. This is the time to give them what they need so that they can live in the world in a good way. That's what I tell the young women when I talk to them about their children and grandchildren.

Yet the government agencies took many of our sacred little beings and put them in boarding schools far, far away. If they died, they didn't even return the child's body to their people, and so whole families died inside. Their loved ones, their sacred little beings, were taken from them, and went somewhere and never came home. Today there's a move to return their remains to their families. One of our ancestors named Little Hawk, who was a cousin to Crazy Horse and who had been buried at the Pennsylvania boarding school where he died, was returned to us not long ago. We had services for him, and his remains were buried with his family. So there's an effort that has begun that's intended to honor our traditions.

The 1883 Code of Indian Offenses[3] was enacted by the United States to outlaw our culture and disrupt the leadership and governance of our tiospaye. It was very successful, leaving very few healthy and strong people to learn, teach, and carry on our traditional way of life. The balance of taking care of each other as healthy families, ones that plan for a good future—this was horribly

---

3 The 1883 Code of Indian Offenses was the central piece in a body of legislation intended to restrict the religious and cultural ceremonies of Native American tribes. Its goal was the complete assimilation and Christianization of American Indians.

disrupted. Over five generations, every one of our families was disrupted.

On our reservation of Pine Ridge, the people experience high rates of every social ill: alcoholism, suicide, infant mortality, incest, sexual abuse, domestic violence, diabetes, unemployment, severely poor nutrition, and more. The effects are multigenerational. Grandmothers are raising their great-grandchildren when the parents are unable, unwilling, or deceased. A woman once told me: "We have to take our grandkids to funerals so they can eat."

This accelerated for our people in 1953 when President Eisenhower repealed Indian prohibition throughout the United States. This made alcohol readily available to our communities. That's when I began to see the deterioration of those very important family ways. The breakdown in family culture started to happen in my lifetime. I saw where parenting fell apart, and responsibility fell to the grandmothers and the grandfathers.

This pushing of alcohol as a way of life was never anything that our people wanted. There have been consequences to this action and our women have suffered greatly. We were getting frightened for our men and of our men. So, it has only been that long since these ideas about the sacredness of women shifted within our culture. This leads me to believe that there is an opportunity to return to our deep traditional respect for matrilineal lines. Our people on Pine Ridge were finally successful in shutting down the sale of alcohol within our community in 2016. This brings me hope.

It has taken many generations to reach this point. It will take many generations to restore our people.

Keeping Our Languages

While other Native children were told not to speak their Native language, no one in my home ever told me that. I do remember feeling strange about it, because in the third grade I was playing with some classmates and talking my language. They stopped and told me, "We understand what you're saying but we can't speak our language. We can't talk with you." I remember thinking, How could you understand what I'm saying and yet you can't talk?

As I grew older, I began to understand that there were families who had suffered the loss of our language by being punished if they spoke it, so they had decided not to teach it to their children. That's why, in some of our more traditional families, the ability to speak the language became very special. Many special things are better communicated in our language, which also contains various shorthand communications. For example, a single word can convey an entire sentence. By comparison, for me the English language is very backward. Throughout my life, I've had to take the English language in, flip it over in my head so that I understand it in my language, then flip it back to express my response in English. As a result, it's hard for me to make flippant remarks because by the time I finish doing all of this, the moment is lost.

Our names, too, are different than our English names. Among my people, I'm not Loretta Afraid of Bear Cook. I'm Anpetu Luta Wi. Loosely translated, it means Red Day Woman, but what it means is that I do everything in the light of the day. I honor that the daytime is sacred, just as the nighttime is sacred. In my Oglala people's way, we have sixteen aspects of God that make up one God: The sun, the sky, the moon, Mother Earth, the night, the day. My special connection is with the day.

Our names, our actual identities, can get lost in bad translation. In our Lakota language, the meaning of our last name is not "Afraid of Bear." My grandfather's name was, in our language, "Even the Bears Are Afraid of This Man."

A Dutiful Path Laid Early

I had a rebellious time in my life also. But at the core—for the most part of my life—I have followed tradition. I have continued always in our Afraid of Bear family ways, which are ours, and that I learned through my family, but they were and are also grounded in the Lakota universe and culture. My aunties, my uncles and grandfathers, they all taught me something. In the way they were, in what they thought about, their humility, in the way they prayed.

As I have grown older, it is my mother and the way that she was that deepens in me. I work to keep alive her teachings, her instructions, her lifelong wisdom, her intuitions.

My uncle Vern American Horse had been adamant with me about this duty very early in my life. I wasn't more than three or four when they took me to have my ears pierced. In our way, that has its ceremony and its instructions. So that way of instruction starts very early. For instance, they told me about keeping track of my earrings and not letting anybody touch them and all of that.

This was constant, in the way they raised me—the Seven Sacred Rites, the different ceremonies. As we recover our practice of these ways, we see the wisdom of our old people.

My Mother, Beatrice

My mother was the greatest influence in my life, and her teachings ring in my mind on most days.

She taught me that food talks and it says, "Whosoever wants to keep me, there is where I will not stay. Whosoever wants to keep giving me away, there is where I will stay." She taught us this because she said that without food or water, we as individuals and communities are not able to grow.

If we have something to share, we are to share it wholeheartedly. She would say, "If you just give truly from your heart and say, 'Here, take it.' That is when the full intent of your gift will be realized." She would say if a pulse jumps into you when you are thinking of giving something to someone, then you did not really want to give it wholeheartedly. If that is the case, then you should not give it at all because the gift becomes a burden. In such cases, the intent of the gift will never be fully realized. The more you push a gift out, the more it is going to keep coming back to you. In this manner, the gifts do not stop coming.

> **"My mother was the greatest influence in my life, and her teachings ring in my mind on most days."**

My mother taught me when to plant, harvest, and prepare ceremonial food according to the cycle of women and the natural world. We cannot do ceremony without sacred food, she told me all my life. She made sure I knew every aspect of how to put our prayers forward. The preparation of the food follows a certain way; we have to complete each element. She was known for her careful preparation of sacred food, and I am humbled to be able to carry on her ways and teach them to others who want to learn.

My mother told us that our women must stay strong and that traditional respect for our matrilineal lines could be reaffirmed, that they were not lost, just misplaced. She told us we have to have the courage to make changes and pull each other up. All is not lost, not yet. This gives me hope.

My mother had that deep wisdom of loving the people and understanding the people, even when they are hard on each other. As our people persisted in practicing our traditional ceremonial ways, the Indian police would come to their homes. Somebody would report to the police that "there are people doing traditional things, back over there in this or that community."

I would wonder to my mother about that, and feel disappointed or even angry at our own people for reporting on each other.

My mother advised me this way:

"It's easy to get angry at our own people. We have feelings inside of us and we don't know where they come from. When we see how all this despair happening, how all these people are angry, we turn it, and there is nowhere to

go with that anger, nowhere to talk about it. So our people turn on each other because that is the only place they can go."

From that point on, I understood better how deep the feelings of anger and despair are here at Pine Ridge, how we have internalized all that anger for generations now. So, I learned not to see our people as "bad" as they act out their suffering and pain.

She also taught that nothing material ever belongs to us. She would say if the Earth Mother wants your body, then you are going to lay out there. If the air wants its air back, it's going to take it back and you are going to lay out there. This extends to our ceremonies. So, when you go into that Sun Dance lodge you are doing it even unto death. You are giving everything that you are for that prayer. You are sharing it with the elements, as even your body is just on loan to you by the Creator. There are many, many hundreds of teachings like this that helped to make up our Lakota way of life.

A Good Man Is a Blessing

My mother told me, "If you have a man in your life you are very blessed. There are not enough good men in the world to go around for every woman." She said those who have a father, a grandfather, those who have a husband, and uncles and sons, are very blessed. There are ceremonies that we have, she said, to honor that.

My husband's people have a tradition. When a man marries, he belongs to his wife's families. I really like that. I decided, when I was faced with it, I said, "Oh, here is the man I am going to marry."

So I married him. Tom Kanatakiente Cook and I have been married over forty years. He and I have built a life that stands on tradition. Sometimes it is hard for us because we are from two different tribes. We are intertribally married. So the enrichment that we can give to our children is the benefit of both sides of these people.

My husband is from the Mohawk people, the Haudenosaunee. I'm Oglala. I had to bring my children into everything so they have exposure into all procedures of tradition. That is how we brought our children up.

My husband and I have been praying together for forty-three years. We tease each other, we laugh, we have a good time, and at the same time, when somebody asks us for prayer, we're there—whether the prayers are for Lakota here on the reservation, or for people in Santiago, Chile, or Nayarit, Mexico. My husband is a Sun Dance leader and a medicine person that I'm honored to walk beside.

The Papal Bulls Deny our Humanity

In 2010, Loretta and her mother, Beatrice, provided testimonies at the Smithsonian Institution on the subject of the Papal Bulls of 1493. This church edict that appears to deny humanity of Indian peoples was a concern of the elder Beatrice, a strong Catholic as well as traditionalist. Beatrice's mandate on this issue propelled the nominee to a meeting with the Pope at the Vatican in 2016, where she was able to express the concern to the Holy Father, and initiate the discussion process within the Church.

My mother respected all religions, and even practiced and attended the Catholic Church on the reservation. But her foundation and instructions for us were grounded in the traditional ceremonial ways. She was our main Sun Dance leader for our family, and danced steadily into her eighties. She knew it all and had lived it all.

As she traveled more of the world, speaking as an elder and woman leader, she became aware of the Doctrine of Discovery, how it had been the justification for the taking of American Indian lands and properties over the centuries. What hurt her most about the doctrine was that the Catholic Church had declared we are people with no souls. She felt most betrayed about the Papal Bulls, how that declaration from 1493 to 1494, had defined Native peoples. She called it the big insult. It was a major teaching of the Catholic Church, to declare Native people as not human for not being Christian.

My mother said we need to bring this to the surface because this to me is the root of all the genocide, and all of the bad things that the non-Native government has put on our people. She said to me, it's in the Christian thinking all over the world, it isn't just here in the United States. She said it is in South America, Central America. It is in Australia. It is all over the world. It is in India, it is in Tibet, and everywhere. They said we were not even human, she said. She would cry about this insult to both her ancestors and her descendants.

I learned so much about how to see the world from my mother, as a woman of my people. As she handled our culture, with her natural ability and intelligence, with her intuitions, it was all a teaching, a constant challenge, and a learning.

The Most Powerful, Sacred Movement

When I address my people formally, I first call on *Skan*, which means Sacred Movement, or the Great Vibration, or Creator. Then I call on the female element, *Wo'ope*, which means "the law of the mother" or "Mother Law." I'm invoking the laws that are specific to women, to the mother spirit, to mitochondrial DNA, which confirms: you are what your mother is. I come from a long line of grandmothers and will pass what I am to my daughters and granddaughters.

The universe is ordered so that planets and people and all beings can move and not create chaos. Women hold a special place in the cosmos because of our receptivity. We're the vessels that stand between heaven and earth. Everything that comes from the cosmos comes through us. Our reproductive years are an especially powerful time: energy comes from the cosmos through us to the earth, and energy comes back from the earth through us to the heavens. In the Oglala way, when a woman is fertile it is a powerful time. When she's pregnant, then she is the most powerful of all.

My grandparents always emphasized the importance of paying attention to our dreams. Such dreams dictated how our nations moved forward, and they dictated our sacred events. When the young women were out in their *isnati*, their mooning time, they were considered very special. This cycle dictated the tribal calendar. Our women had a great influence in the direction of the nations and helped to determine what the community had to do within that twenty-eight-day time frame.

I think today the Western culture has steered our women away from this. For us, our moon time was never considered a sick time and it never carried the stigma that is does for Western societies. Rather, it was understood that we were at our most powerful time because we were getting our bodies ready to be the recipient of a man's gift. As birthing nations, it was critical to give back to the women and acknowledge each of the things that were important in the female world.

There is a vocabulary I associate with my woman teachers and their lifelong instruction:

wahwoptetusni: steadfast, one of a kind, hard to find another just like her

shakica: physically strong and beautiful to behold in everything she does

waglu eatapi: sacred food offering ceremony prayer

These words represent what I strive to be, what many young women say they want to become. Because I believe them and believe in them, I want to share my lived experiences, knowledge, and wisdom.

SACRED FOOD

Our traditional foods are sacred, and we developed with them and their sources in the natural world over thousands of years. Some are very special, and at different occasions, and for specific ceremonies, they are prepared in special ways. All of our spiritual ways are guided and enriched by the practice of our sacred foods and our sacred foods enrich all of our ceremonies. They help us even in time of death.

Wherever a relative of ours is buried, we bury them with sacred food. That sacred food goes by the season. It is water for the winter. Corn for the spring. Cherries for the summer. Meat for the fall. When you bury your loved one with the sacred food, you put it in their hand and they go to the spirit world to give that to the Creator. That is our gift through our loved one to the Creator, because now they see the Creator's face.

Toss the Ball

About ten years ago, when one of my mothers reached eighty-two years old, she came and said to me, "I have my fifth generation now, and I want to do one of the seven ceremonies, the one that we call 'Toss the Ball.'"

When she had asked around about the ceremony, searching for people who could do it faithfully, she said other elders told her to come and ask me. I was really taken aback because I did not think of myself particularly as such a knowledgeable person in these ways. I was thinking to myself, This is how far we have come in losing these things?

Her request, of course, her intuition for the proper time to do things, is always part of my own continuing growth, moving me to realize even more about how beautiful my culture is.

In looking to help arrange for this elder's Toss the Ball ceremony, I realized that important pieces were missing. Most people had not learned those ways as children. Being in it all my life, it had not been all that noticeable to me how fragile our way of life had become.

My uncle Vern mentions in his interview for the American Horse archives how the grandfathers told him that our people were gifted by the Creator with the knowledge of the Seven Rites. It is our responsibility to remember them and to practice them, now and again, as we can, even in these modern times.

I realized more clearly that not every family was doing these things. And it hurt my feelings because I was thinking, No wonder we are in such a state of chaos. And that continuance of everything sacred and everything human in our everyday lives was being done in very few families. I felt, no wonder we could not understand the breakdown in our societies. I realized that was a big reason.

In searching to perform the Toss the Ball ceremony for my mother, when we looked at the singing of the songs and the procedural ways of those elements, we found that they were very obscure. They were almost hidden. We had to search for answers by going back through ceremony.

We made a ceremony in the dark. We covered the windows and didn't let any light in. We sat with the Medicine Man and we asked for that spirit that he calls in—an eagle spirit. He comes and doctors our people. He gives forth information, speaking in a sacred language called Hanbloglaka. So, in that ceremony, I asked the spirit about it.

What does "toss the ball" mean?

He said, speaking in Hanbloglaka, it is a way to revere that a woman is arriving at her later age, like with your mother, her path to full womanhood is done. In that line of respect, that this woman is now a co-creator. She is next to the Creator. It is in the context, he said, that you and all begin to understand how important this woman is.

Receiving such knowledge, through ceremony, is very strong. It reveals there are different ways to seek our spirituality and the knowledge of our ceremonies.

Last Sacred Rite

I have completed the last sacred rite—keeping of my own mother's soul. In that sacred space, the sacred food is required. My mother left me on March 18, 2016, at age eighty-eight. In keeping with her careful instruction, I made prayer requests that are just a little different from those we make every day. I asked her spirit that was still here with us to take an offering of *wasna*, or sacred food, to the Creator—water, small bits of corn, chokecherries, and buffalo meat.

Our prayer is always that we accept that she will see the Creator's face and that she will intervene on our behalf to help our people. At the thanksgiving feast and giveaway, we fed her soul for the last time, made releasing prayers, and acknowledged all the people who took care of us during the time of her death.

I thank Skan and Wo'ope every day for having her as my mother. I use her teachings every day. I'm a better human being for her teachings. I miss her very much.

Keeping Our Ways Alive

Not enough of our people have a way to learn our culture. Back in the day, the churches, the government said we weren't supposed to have any of it. A lot of people went into hiding, doing their ceremonies sometimes but in individual families, and so a lot of the songs went unheard and unused, and the procedural ways were partly lost.

This happened not because we did not think them important, but because you had to hide. When you know your hands are going to get slapped, when you get insulted and punished for speaking your mother's language…well, that makes it hard to be yourself. And we needed to be ourselves. We needed to be who we are. So we kept it alive. Our way threads the spiritual currents with our worldly lives. In this connection, the memory of everything still lives. If we just do it, we'll remember how to do it.

Not only are we in danger of losing some of our cultural traditions if the younger generation is not given the opportunity to learn these teachings, we are in danger of losing many of our sacred foods due to climate change, pollution, and the Western culture's misunderstanding about the importance of balance in nature.

My grandparents and parents taught me early on that food sovereignty is a critical component to having a vibrant, healthy, and thriving community or nation. As the world is changing and the effects of attempted genocide have shown themselves to have caused great damage to our communities, it is time to reclaim our place as the strong Nation and caretakers of Unci Maka that we are as Oglala people. The Western systems are failing, as our ancestors warned that they would.

We need to educate the younger generation, our people, and the world about the importance of language, traditional knowledge, and sacred foods, clear air and water, and our cultures and traditions. These are not simply "quaint ideas," as many in the Western culture like to believe. They were developed based upon our own sciences by highly trained master teachers (Native scientists). The more we can provide examples of this, the more our own people can understand the value and strength of their heritage. The more they understand this, the more they will defend it and take the time to learn it and reincorporate it into their lives once again.

I had ceremony around me, the ritualization, the continuance of that. There were no breaks in how we attended ceremony, even though we weren't fully, legally, recognized to practice outwardly until twenty-five years ago with the American Indian Religious Freedom Act.[4] That federal law came to bear that we could come out and celebrate who we were. Today we need the government to recognize that we have a wise and ancient religious way. We have our spirituality. We go back thousands of years. If we didn't have those survival skills, as community, we wouldn't be here today. No matter what family you come from, they have merit. They have good things to teach. You wouldn't be here but your family brought you here. You're survivors, we're all survivors. No matter

---

4 The American Indian Religious Freedom Act of 1978 protects the rights of Native American people to exercise their traditional religions by ensuring access to sites, use and possession of sacred objects, and the freedom to worship through ceremonials and traditional rites.

who we are, what tribe we belong to. In each of those tribal nations we belong to, we have our own ways.

The Good Road to Truth

I'm a grandmother now. When I look back on my life, I ask myself, "Did I take good care of my sacred pipe? Have I offered the rites of passage to my children and grandchildren? Have I been participating in *inipi* (sweat lodge)? Have I completed a vision quest? Have I honored my dead with the keeper of the soul ceremony?"

These questions continue the thoughts and concerns my mother carried.

When you're raised with respect for creation like that, it's hard to watch what is happening to the earth and not be alarmed. These times are trying for us because we all need to get along, and yet we also need to realize that humans are here for such a very short time. It's incredibly presumptuous of us to destroy the earth in a span of only a couple of hundred years. We humans are just a breath of air in the millennia of creation. We hold that air just for a little while, and then we go on. When we're ready for the next dimension, we give our breath back to the air and go—nothing to be afraid of. It's hard to let go of life when it's so beautiful, yet my people believe we're here to advance a process that's been going on for thousands of years. We're given this gift of life and should nurture and take care of it as much as we can—across all peoples and clans, collaborating with their ancestral knowledge and ways as much as we can.

"If enough of us stand up to share, teach, and support, the good road to truth, compassion, and health will appear more clearly before us."

As a mother and a grandmother, it is very important to me that I create a map for my loved ones to follow, if they so choose. I also wish to help those who do not have parents or grandparents to mentor them in these very important ways. It is hard to walk forward in a good way when you do not have a solid, foundational understanding of who and what you are. As Oglala Lakota people, our traditional stories and lifeways help to teach us who we are, where we come from, and where we will ultimately return to. The colonizing force worked hard to take these teachings away from us. As a result, we see the struggles around us and within our communities today. However, if enough of us stand up to share, teach, and support, the good road to truth, compassion, and health will appear more clearly before us. Then we can simply decide to step upon it and follow it. For me, to see more of this in my lifetime provides great personal healing.

I Stand in My Truth

White Buffalo Calf Woman brought the seven sacred rites to the women but told us we were to share our gifts, her teachings, with the men. After two hundred years of colonization and persecution, some of these ways have been lost to some of the people; they could go to jail for practicing them. I'm old enough to remember having uncles and grandfathers being taken to jail. So now it's my job to teach our ways again, very lovingly.

I feel privileged to have known major teachers among my people and culture. In trying to follow their deepest instructions, I have lived many revealing and instructive experiences, not a few adventures, many heartbreaks, and countless uplifting moments.

I am very excited about connecting with other Indigenous women. Collectively we are the thread and the weavers of social transformation in our communities. Working together and sharing ceremonial space with women is not luck or coincidence. It is clear to me that it is meant to be, that our power intensifies when we come together in prayer.

> *"My grandfather George Sword said, 'These things are for us to give; they're not for us to keep.'"*

It is important that the work we get involved in is documented so the teachings that come from it are accessible. In my Lakota culture, each leader of the tiospaye had a winter count. They referenced significant events within a given time period. These recordings supplemented our oral traditions and history, and helped to mark our journey together as people. I envision the legacy of our women leaders their many ways of continuing this important practice.

The more culture bearers open our hearts and minds, the more accessible the knowledge inside becomes to those seeking their path. The values I adhere to—courage, generosity, humility, love for our people—make transference of knowledge, cultural survival, and social transformation possible. This is the only way to move forward together and intact. My elder relatives held the same values and lived the same purpose, and now I am in the position to apply it for our people because of what I learned from them. As my Grandfather George said, "These things are for us to give; they're not for us to keep."

It is the truth I have stood in all my life.

"We're all sent into this life with something powerful to give."

WAKÉRAKATS:TE LOUISE HERNE
Akwesasne Mohawk

WAKÉRAKATS:TE LOUISE HERNE is a traditionalist leader and consistent innovator who illuminates the journey of her people to regenerate love for themselves, their children, and their ancestral culture.

Her lifelong home community is the Akwesasne Mohawk Reservation, which straddles the US-Canadian border on the St. Lawrence River. A Bear Clan Mother in the traditional Longhouse, she pulls the threads of ancient matrilineal knowledge from Sky Woman's original legacy to the present. Louise activates ceremony as a way of being and knowing over the life course—truly as a pathway away from violence and abuse, and from illness to health. For over a decade, she has led young people and their relations through *Ohero:kon*, a four-year rite of passage to contemplate and steadily incorporate Haudenosaunee values that will guide them as adults. Through her Moon Lodge Society, Louise opens sacred space linked to natural cycles for girls and women, a place where prophetic dreams are shared and made real.

Louise brings her knowledge and traditional standing in the institution of Mother Law to help develop a responsible future for our people.[1] Always starting from a place of perpetual gratitude, a foundational Longhouse teaching, she has co-created a renewed

---
[1] Kahnistensera

Haudenosaunee narrative for resilience and resistance. Louise embodies the head Corn Mother spirit of keeping her hand on the heart of her people.

Louise received an honorary degree of doctor of humane letters from the State University of New York in 2017.

IAKOIANE

I'm a condoled Bear Clan Mother of the Kanien'kehá:ka, the People of the Flint. We are known as the Eastern Doorkeepers of the Haudenosaunee, or the People of the Longhouse. My home is Akwesasne, a place of complex and multilayered jurisdictions.[2] I am enrolled with the Mohawks of Akwesasne on our northern side, and with the Saint Regis Mohawk on our southern end. My ancestral identity and citizenship lies with the Mohawk Nation.[3]

I am a third-generation Iakoiane, and keeper of the traditional Haudenosaunee bear clan chieftainship title Tehanákarí:ne since 2005.[4] In our Longhouse ways, it is a woman who possesses the title of chieftainship, the power to name a chief; this right is in

---

2 The Akwesasne Mohawk people are located in a reservation community that straddles the US-Canadian border on the St. Lawrence River, and intersects the provinces of Ontario and Quebec and the state of New York. The Mohawk people sustain under multiple jurisdictions and three Indigenous-tribal governmental entities, including Canadian and US elective systems and traditional Longhouse government.

3 Titles of clan mothers or chiefs in the traditional Longhouse are formalized by the "Condolence Ceremony." Thus she or he was said to be "seated" for life, and fully "condoled."

4 *Iakoiane*, meaning "it belongs to her," refers to the title belonging to a woman leader of a family group, or clan. *Tehanákarí:ne* refers to the Lead Bear Clan Chief title.

honor of Tsiókonsah:se, the Seneca woman who was first to accept the Peacemaker's strategy for ending war among the early Haudenosaunee. She is known as the Mother of Nations. For this reason, clan mothers alone hold the authority to raise chiefs.

An Early Vision

I grew up on a farm in Tsi snaihne.[5] One spring day when I was three years old, my mother sent me out to play while she worked in the house. As I was walking out the door, she instructed me to stay away from the barn. I said okay and walked toward the front yard until she stopped watching me. Then I made a big loop around some trees and made a beeline for the barn.

Behind the barn was a shoddy staircase that went up to a loft about fourteen feet high. Up in the loft, my family kept household items and assorted farm tools—leather horse harnesses, maple sugar taps, and pails. I climbed those rickety stairs and reached the old blue door at the top. It had no handle or knob, just a rope made of bailing twine that was tied to a nail on the frame to keep it closed. I unhooked the twine and pushed the door open to look around at all the treasures.

All of a sudden, I heard my mother calling for me. I ran to the door and grabbed the twine as I rushed out. I pulled it really hard to shut the door, but it got stuck so I gave it another, harder tug. It snapped. There was no rail around that little landing where the staircase connected to the barn, and I fell off it.

---

5 Tsi snaihne is an area within the northern portion of Akwesasne.

I knew there was a huge rock below the landing and I was waiting to hit it. Then I felt something grab me under my armpits. I was lifted back up to that high loft and stood up on my feet. When I turned around, I saw this magnificent, illuminated lady with huge wings. I felt her pure love; it felt like ten times the way my mother loved me (and I always knew my mother loved me). Even now I remember that feeling. It was so powerful. She was so beautiful. As I studied her, she dissipated into the sky and then I made my way back down the stairs.

I hid that memory for a long time because I didn't know if it was real. It's not until now that I know that it's possible, and it's real.

Growing up Rough

In my growing years there was a lot of domestic violence. I witnessed a lot of trauma. My sisters often say that because I was the baby of the family I didn't see half of what they had seen. My father was a World War II veteran. He was an alcoholic. He carried the war in his head every day. Eventually he drank himself to death. I think it was the post-traumatic stress disorder from the war and what he had experienced there that made him so mean. There was always a lot of violence between him and my mom. That was unfortunate, because when he was sober he was a pretty nice guy.

Fifty years ago, here in Akwesasne, it was a different world than how we're living now. It was really tough, the conditions I grew up in—no running water, no electricity. Our food came from our hard work in the fields, and the hunting and fishing that had to be done.

As a child I watched my father and other family members slowly die from their addictions. I always knew that our community, including myself, needed healing. I felt a strong urge to change the experience because I didn't want my children to grow up in a violent, alcoholic home like I did. I didn't want it to be the norm. So I fought really hard to bring sobriety into my home, and to embed our language in the consciousness of my children and now my grandchildren. It was important to me to change the story that our children and the future generations will inherit.

Becoming Clan Mother

The story of how I became a clan mother begins two centuries ago. In the late 1800s, my grandmother Mary Jacobs Gabriel was taken from our community at the age of six to attend Shingwauk Indian Residential School in Sault Ste. Marie. She didn't return until she was eighteen years old. She returned able to read and write but she lost a lot of who she was. My grandmother married very young, at eighteen or nineteen, and had ten children. My mother was her oldest daughter.

At the turn of the twentieth century, and into the 1930s, there was a resurgence of the Longhouse tradition among the Haudenosaunee. There was a movement by the Confederacy to replant the titles among the Mohawks, to uphold the principles of the Great Law of Peace.[6]

---

6 The Great Law of Peace, a central oral foundation of the ancient League of the Haudenosaunee, or the League of Six Nations, which united the eastern woodlands confederacy of Mohawk, Oneida, Onondaga, Cayuga, Seneca, and, later, Tuscarora.

At that time they went through the Native communities. Among Mohawks, it was Akwesasne, and our two sister communities of Kahnawà:ke and Kanehsatà:ke just down the St. Lawrence River. They were looking for families that still had the language, "to plant young saplings" to see if the old chieftain titles would grow.

This movement took root in my family. My grandmother Mary Jacobs Gabriel was approached for a clan mother role. She researched her clan family and found that she fit the criteria for the position. She eventually agreed to accept the strands of wampum and, with them, the responsibilities of tending to the title.

I remember falling asleep beside my mother in a Longhouse ceremony at Kanehsatà:ke when I was about three years old. It was 1963. I didn't understand why we were there or what was going on, but it seemed to have real importance. Years later, I learned that event was the Condolence ceremony for my grandmother and her eldest son.[7] She had raised his name for the title of Tehanákarí:ne.

When my grandmother died in the early 1970s, my mother, the oldest of five daughters, accepted her wampum strands at her ten-day feast. She went through small condolence in the 1980s. When she died, my sisters decided that I was the only one who was eligible to fill her position as clan mother: I spoke our language, I was married to someone of the opposite clan, and I had daughters. So at my mother's feast, the late wolf clan sub-chief Jake Swamp did the ceremonial words and he handed me my mother's wampum.

---

7 The Condolence ceremony is an ancient ritualized procedure to clear the mind and senses of grief and sadness over the loss of a chief. A condoled leader is raised up ceremonially and witnessed by the people.

I held onto my mother's strands for nine years. At the time I was a really young mother with five children. I couldn't imagine taking on a political life. The responsibility was too enormous for anyone to carry. I spent a lot of time researching the other titles. I was so willing to give it to another family because who wants to carry the burden of a nation? Still, I had a really strong obligation to my mother and my grandmother because they sacrificed and suffered in order to make that Haudenosaunee women's tradition live. I was not going to be the broken link in the chain or be the one to sever the root they planted.

"A power greater than ourselves is the guiding force to all the women's work that is now being done in our community."

Louise Herne, Haudenosaunee Faithkeeper Oren Lyons, Katsi Cook and Alexandra David

Around the ninth year, the wampum started talking to me. Every time I was looking for something around my house, the strands would surface. It started to tug at my will and tug at my consciousness. One day, I was approached by a wolf clan chief. He said the Nation was calling for a Condolence ceremony and asked if I was ready to put up leaders. My thoughts were, Well…we're not a perfect family and we're riddled with historical trauma just like anyone else, but I'll put my best candidates forward.

Aronhiaies, my oldest son, was the one that emerged. He was only nineteen at the time. He was brought up in ceremony and Longhouse ways and he was fluent in the language, so I moved him forward so I moved him forward as a sub-chief. I borrowed from another bear clan family and sat Curtis Nelson as the older chief.

We were condoled into leadership at the Mohawk Nation longhouse here in Akwesasne. During the ritual of condolence, I stared out at the pouring rain beating against the window and said a silent prayer to the Creator:

Sonkwaiatison, I don't know why you stood me up here. I am the weakest in all of your creation. I know so little of how it is to be a woman leader among my people. I know even less of how to watch over a chief. But you, Creator of all things on earth, stood me here. If I am to fulfill the duties of Iakoiane and uphold a life of peace and nobility, then I impart a most desperate request: help me.

Since that moment and prayer, I know I have been greeted by spiritual beings. I often feel guided to the headwaters of ancestral knowledge. A power greater than ourselves is the guiding force to all the women's work that is now being done in our community.[8]

Ceremonial Passage

When my oldest daughter was coming into what I call the moon time, her bleeding time, I didn't ever want her to feel shame about it. I wanted to ritualize it. I went about asking, interviewing, and reading about how to celebrate my daughter's moon time.

This was the initial motivation for reconstructing the puberty rite for young women. Then, at one of the first ceremonies I did for

---

8 Wakerakatste, in Jeanette Rodriguez, "A Clan Mother's Call: Reconstructing Haudenosaunee Cultural Memory," SUNY Press, 2017, and editors' interview.

a young woman, her uncles asked me, What about the boys, what is there for them? From there I was catapulted into performing a ceremonial puberty rite, a coming of age for both girls and boys that evolved into Ohero:kon.[9]

Ohero:kon came through a lot of work—gathering of the old ways, talking among our people, interviews, praying, and trusting in the gut to reconstruct what we needed. Of course, I wasn't alone. I had a lot of help from my family and community. I was fortunate that people trusted me to venture down this path. Beloved sisters in my community helped me build this work.

It has developed into our movement to respond to the loss of our culture. That destruction of culture, the tearing apart of our families and our relationship with the land, is all part of colonization that continues even to this day. Our struggle is to continuously rebuild from that by gathering our youth and nurturing them onto a deeper cultural path, to one that was stolen from their ancestors.

Ohero:kon is a full process that starts around our Midwinter ceremonies with weekly gatherings at our longhouse for shared Indigenous knowledge and workshops. It culminates over four ceremonial days in late spring, where the nieces and nephews retreat in isolation and silence into the woods to fast and pray, and seek vision from one to four days depending on their "year." Their core helpers —chosen aunties and uncles, mothers and other relatives—keep watch over their fasting sites day and night.

---

9 *Ohero:kon* in Mohawk means "under the husk" and is an annual adolescent rite-of-passage ceremonial process conducted at Akwesasne.

It's a really intimate and peaceful time. On the last day the young people are reunited with their families, then celebrated with a community feast. To me, it's just a beautiful sight to see our young people lined up in their finest clothing and bursting with pride for themselves and each other. It's a great healing for all of us.

It is heartfelt and done with purpose. It's also rigorous and demanding, and yet the young people keep coming every year. Some years we've had as many as seventy initiates from our own nation at Akwesasne and from other reservation communities and tribes. We've welcomed many visitors from Indian families and nations who come to help out and see how they can do something similar from their own culture. These include people from Onondaga, Seneca, Oneida, Cree, Cherokee, Lakota, from the United States, Canada—even Indigenous people from Latin America and many others. Some have carried out their ideas about how to conduct this process of a ceremonial rite of passage in their home cultures and communities.

The young adult participant in her or his fast and time of isolation must be supported by four adults from her or his family circle. These are adults she or he invites to help guide and advise and assist her or him in undertaking their prayer, songs, sweat lodge, and fasting vision quest. Helping and offering your best advice by four adults opens and reopens many relationships. It's a serious commitment to the young person. This is the deepest healing, often for the whole family circle.

We're approaching twenty-one years of Ohero:kon, of using our cultural knowledge to recreate a puberty rite for adolescents. I think that's where the story begins to change. Now we are giving attention to the important points where monumental change needs to occur as our young people walk into adulthood. It's important, because before those young adolescents become parents themselves, we elders must direct which way the winds blow. It was really important that the narrative change.

Healing in Families

There are miraculous moments in the work I do with young women. One that sticks with me is when I was working with an adolescent girl probably about the age of fifteen. Her parents had divorced and she hadn't seen her father since she was eight because the breakup was really difficult. As part of her ritual she stood across the fire from her father so he could speak to her. It was a really intense moment because you could see every muscle in her face tense up when he arrived. You could see the feelings of anger, abandonment, and resentment in her. Her body was stiff and rejecting his presence. It was really a hard space to be in. But he showed up!

He stood across the fire from her and he said, "When you were eight, I left your mother and I didn't realize that I left you, too. In my own selfishness I haven't been there for the last eight years of your life." He said, "From this day forward, I promise I'll be present. I want to be present, I want to be there for all the milestones in your life." He said, "I've always loved you since you were born, but it's because of my own selfishness and my own stubbornness that I didn't see how much I had hurt you."

With each word that he spoke, she slowly started to melt. She started to cry, and by the time he finished his address to her, she forgave him and just about jumped into his arms. It was so beautiful to witness because it brought them back together. I get emotional because it's real. You can't get more bared truth than that, to stand in front of healing that's going on between a father and his daughter.

When you reach that level, that depth in the human condition and emotion and healing, that's real. No doctor can prescribe that. It's something you have to enact and must have the courage to carry through. To this day I applaud that father who showed up and the daughter who accepted her father's presence. To me that's the miracle.

Youth Is Energy

These young people have opened up my mind. Our longhouse is very gendered. The way we are seated has a very specific male/female dynamic. As part of the healing of our community, a lot of our young people have found the courage to emerge as queer, gay, transgender, lesbian. I have to listen and open up my mind to the reemergence of that medicine society within our community and I have to create space for them. We can't afford to throw them away. There has to be inclusion. We have to include them in all aspects of our culture and community.

I sit and listen to their stories and welcome them. They're still our children. That was a huge door to open. I grew up with the narrative that it's either man or woman, there's nothing else. I've begun to understand more profoundly that there is something else. It's not even a choice; you're just born into this wonderful spectrum of wanting to love somebody and wanting to be loved. Everybody should be allowed to love who they want to love. That's one of the things that really matters that I had to open my mind up to.

Youth to me is simply energy, like mountains of energy, even like a raging river. It's energy that needs to be guided. Working with young people, you can really be inspired to accomplish something. Their energy has fueled my ability to be expressive, to be creative, and also to have the courage to research and to go above and beyond the usual narrative that we're given. Being able to witness this metamorphosis, it sticks with you forever. It's just beautiful.

Guidance, Not Rescue

First and foremost is the ability to listen to our young women, to hear them, see where they're at and see what it is that they need, then to create the space for them to reach the capacity of their full expression of self. I'm refining the skill of not trying to rescue our young women. When she's going through something really hard and is struggling, I'll listen. I may give advice but I don't go in and rescue anymore. It took me a while to recognize that if I'm doing the work and I'm doing the rescuing, then it's for me, not her. Whenever I work with someone—and it's not just women; I've worked with men, too—I try and just guide their thinking to a different place. I don't tell them what to do. I try to get them to think through what they're doing. Try and see if they can do it differently.

With a traumatized young person, I try to connect her to something greater than herself. I might immediately connect her to the medicines of our Mother Earth and then take her to the earth, connect her there energetically, connect her to the moon, to the sky, and the water. Like our blood, water is a life-giving force, too. I would connect her to something greater than herself and embrace her in the energy and power of Creation. Then I would reposition her inside the universe as something really small within the universe with the ability to create something really big. All things can be overcome. Support her and love her until she can love herself.

I was working with a man who was having marital troubles. He was trying to rationalize the troubles in his marriage and kind of putting all the blame on her and not owning any part of it. I asked him, what part do you play in the disruption of your marriage? How about some ownership? It didn't take him long before he broke down. Helping him recognize what he contributed into the ill will inside their marriage. I tried to talk him into a place of understanding that pattern he established, of doing the same thing with her and getting the same result. What could he do different in order to reach her into a softer, gentler way? Because women need to be treated gently. How about a grand gesture? How about some flowers or maybe a walk in the woods, something different? Trying to change the perspective of the situation from a different point of view. I try to empower them to fix it themselves. That, along with the medicines, helps our people become full participants in their own healing and to their own empowerments.

BLOOD AND VOICE

In a very primordial, human woman way, blood is power. It's powerful for a young woman to understand her blood and her cycle, and to love it. To embrace the power of what it is, and what it holds. If we can get a young girl to embrace that power and move into a place of celebration and personal centering, it could stir a great evolution in her psyche. Blood is life, blood is power. It also comes with voice. I envision what it would be like to have our entire community understand that women are multifaceted creatures and that we should embrace their powers and not ridicule them or diminish them.

From my lived experience, leadership is being unafraid to use your voice. We've sat in silence for a really long time, watched atrocities and violence go on. In certain moments, we've normalized it. When there's something amiss, young women need to use their voices, to project that power and not to be silent. My biggest worry is that women sit in silence. Silence breeds violence.

I grew up in the longhouse. I remember elder women who'd get up and voice their opinion, no holds barred. They were very vocal in council. When I became a clan mother and had to sit in council, I was astounded by the shift from what I remembered. Then, women standing up to speak was the norm. Now, the women were silent. I would wonder, Why are they not saying anything? Eventually, this narrative emerged that clan mothers don't speak. Instead, her voice—her opinions, ideas, criticism—went through the men. To me that was really concerning.

I sit with the chiefs and I still deal with that. It became a narrative within our culture to silence the women. True enough, there are moments when the chiefs need to speak for the people. However, when the women are not even asked for their opinion, that's concerning. That breeds violence, and I wrestle with it.

That's why I'm huge on changing the narrative and encouraging young women to gain proficiency, to project their voices and experiences into the community. To contribute to the story we're going to leave to the younger generations, we have to be present and we have to be vocal.

What I would pay to have a piece of writing from my grandmother or my great-grandmother! Just to know what their experience was, what they went through, the advice they'd have for us. My mother didn't speak English, only Kanien'kehá:ka. She left me a different kind of wealth in terms of understanding the land and understanding the medicines and the language. It's a whole different way of thinking.

I often feel alone and not understood because my thinking can be different. When I think inside our language, for example with our Ohènton Karihwatéhkwen, I address Creation and say, bring to us what we need to know this day.[10] I acknowledge our Mother Earth, the Moon, the Creator and Creation. I say, We're working really hard down here. We're trying to find the right words to empower, recreate, and reconstruct who we once were into a really good place

---

10 *Ohènton Karihwatéhkwen* means "the words that come before all else" and is a Haudenosaunee greeting to the natural world.

again and to recognize the potency of what that was. To help our young women feel pride within themselves again. I say wrap us all up and let us hit the target today.

ALLIANCE OF WOMEN

In all cultures, women are overlooked for positions of power. If we diminish the female power, then it brings a lack of nourishment and nurturing for the future generations. I'm about empowering women to return to positions of prominence. I'm devoted to that, especially in young Indigenous women. Eventually we are going to leave and somebody's going to take over. If we don't give them our love and attention, we handicap them—especially in terms of reproducing culture and language. So we help them rise. We're all sent into this life with something powerful to give. We encourage them to embrace their own individuality and their own gifts. As women, we must return to a place of prominence and empowerment. That's where my passion lies. I want to someday know that I've impacted young women to lead their own generation into a future that belongs to them.

I've always had this vision of a global alliance of powerful women of different nations converging to create a ceremony together for the protection of our Mother. All of us come in the original essence of our woman deities: Sky Woman, White Buffalo Calf Woman, Ever Changing Woman. Women from all over the world gathering to remember our stories of origin, and lifting ourselves through ceremony into a better state of consciousness. We are grappling with the many issues at this moment: a pandemic, a climate crisis, racial injustice. We can rise for the greater good of all humanity.

We've been positioned as authorities over the land. At the time of the establishment of the Great Law of Peace, under the words of Deganawidah and Hiawatha and Tsiókonsah:se, it was established that generations of children would unify under their mothers through the clan system. The clan system was already established prior to the coming of the Great Law, which structures our system of chiefs. The Peacemaker took the sisterhood and put the brotherhood with it, and they were supposed to work in tandem together. In his speech when those first eleven chiefs were condoled, he said their authority will come from the women. The land will belong to the women; therefore any decision about the land will come from the women.

The land is ours and we have to walk it like we own it. Anywhere that I move about in our Native land, I always say I'm the host; most people are guests. We must raise our women of Onkwéhon:we nations to remind visitors who have crossed the great salt water that their ancestors came here as guests and that we're the hosts. We have to develop that narrative to be more consistent and repetitive. In any meeting or in any circle that we meet we need to always remind ourselves that we're not the lesser people here on this continent, and they are visitors here.

The continuity of the generations belongs to the women and the title of the lands belongs to the women. Leadership on these lands belongs to the women and, unless we repeat and repeat that narrative, it's not going to be. Men need to be reminded that they're the voice but they're not the authority. As women we have to be unified. We can't be in competition with each other.

"We have to steady ourselves and prepare for the time when the world comes to our doorstep and asks for help."

I'm just trying to pay it forward, the gift that I'm trying to give to young women. There's a lot we need to contribute to the world and our voices are just breaking the glass ceiling of this capitalist system we live in. We have to steady ourselves and prepare for the time when the world comes to our doorstep and asks for help. Part of readying ourselves is mentoring women into places of personal power and connected knowing, to consider a young woman-mother's time as the most valuable, to permeate her consciousness with steady doses of truth and resilience, to help her recognize her own gifts and her own power.

When it's time, she will stand in her own truth and her own power with no apology.

"I am a work in progress continually coiling myself with the hope of becoming a whole vessel."

NORA NARANJO-MORSE
Kha'p'o Owenge

Contemporary artist and poet NORA NARANJO-MORSE instinctually infuses a resilient ancestral sensibility from her rugged Santa Clara Pueblo homeland into her art. Deeply influenced by her parents' Tewa worldview, Nora has been immersed in the spiritual practices that contribute to becoming a complete human being. Her central commitment is the generational transfer of both ancient and contemporary tribal experience, the sum of many fleeting moments that create identity and culture.

An expressive hands-on learner and educator, Nora favors earth-based materials like glittering micaceous clay and adobe. She also sees potential in more uncommon media, including discard that can be repurposed into meaningful art. Nora's work can be found at the Heard Museum in Phoenix, the Minneapolis Institute of Art, and the National Museum of the American Indian in Washington, DC. Her impactful public art piece at NMAI, "Always Becoming," in many ways exemplifies Nora's preference for knowledge transmission: interactive, collaborative, and benefiting from collective stewardship. Every year the circle that tends to "Always Becoming" widens, as Nora intentionally entrusts volunteers with the caretaking and renewal of her art.

Nora received an honorary doctorate degree from Skidmore College in 2007.

A Tewa Sense of Self and Place

I am a Tewa Pueblo woman from Kha'p'o Owenge, more commonly known as Santa Clara Pueblo. My Tewa name is Wha-Povi, or Spinach Flower. My English name is Lenora Naranjo-Morse.

Tewa people have inhabited the arid land of northern New Mexico since time immemorial. The belief of Kha'p'o centers on our emergence and continued relationship with the earth. Traditional homes, ovens, and even our utilitarian and ceremonial vessels are created from mud and clay from the land. Our traditional values emphasize an awareness of the human as a spiritual being. Through ceremonies, our sense of self and place within the Pueblo world connects us to the seasons, the clouds above us, and the breath that moves in and out of us. We are, by tradition, a matriarchal society. Ceremonies are a time for Kha'p'o to seek spirituality, a symbolic gesture of renewal for the world, ourselves, and others.

Our community is small. Our land base is less than 100,000 acres. The population of Kha'p'o is about 8,000 community members, with tribal enrollment continually growing. Like other Indigenous communities, we face many challenges. We struggle to balance cultural values that are often at odds with the larger society's demands and standards. We face issues of acculturation that tear at the fabric of our families and community. And yet, we are still here and moving forward to build a place for the next generation of Kha'p'o.

When Spanish conquistadors entered the Pueblo world, there were an estimated 200,000 Pueblo people. By the end of the 1800s, half of that estimated Pueblo population had been wiped out by disease and violent death. Pueblo people have a long history of historical trauma because of colonization.

Mesa Verde circa 2019

My mother repeated this story the elders told her of those dark days:

We called the Spanish "Queh Kuu" because of their metal armor. When the Queh Kuu came into the Pueblo, they gathered everyone from the village and herded them to the edge of P'osongeh, the Rio Grande. Standing along the river, a priest took a large cottonwood branch, dipped it into the river and sprinkled everyone, saying words no one understood. The priest baptized everyone in the village with "holy" water. Kha'p'o people thought they were being witched, so they cried out, rolling in the sand along the riverbank, trying to get the evil off of them. When the soldiers saw the resistance, the people were beaten.

One of the physical remnants of colonization is present in the center of every Pueblo plaza throughout the Southwest. Catholic churches built by Pueblo laborers represent a forced belief system that dramatically changed the culture and religious fabric of Pueblo life. The result for contemporary Pueblo people is an ongoing attempt to reconcile Kha'p'o belief with Catholicism and the harsh history of colonization. Not only was there assimilation of our minds, but our spirits as well. Kha'p'o people have learned to adapt. This is evident on ceremonial days when dancers, who've spent weeks in the *kiva*, make a pilgrimage to the Catholic church before the ceremonies begin.

A Corn People

For a younger generation of Kha'p'o, corn planting and harvesting is a seasonal tradition for many Pueblo families. In a cultural and spiritual way, we are a corn people. Corn—*khuun* in Tewa—is woven into our lives in many ways.

There are growing fields on tribal lands below the village near the Rio Grande. The fields are a more community-oriented area where generations of Kha'p'o have grown their food. Corn is the main crop, although people also grow alfalfa and vegetables. The fields have a long and important history to our people. During contemporary times families use the fields to grow food, house cattle and horses, and in the cooler parts of the day, walk for exercise.

"With climate change, our growing seasons have shifted even in my lifetime."

When I am asked how this process of planting and harvesting impacts young women, I think it is reconnecting them back to the earth and to their people. By taking the time to go down to the fields there is separation from technology, and a commitment to a more agrarian traditional Pueblo worldview. It really is an opportunity to reconnect to the land, water, and seasonal cycles. To spend time in the fields is healing and life affirming.

These fields are a resource for younger Kha'p'o, and as more younger women get involved in growing their own foods, they are empowered by ancestral knowledge of land and ways of survival even now. When fifteen bushels of corn have been harvested, the question became: How do we store this food source for the winter?

This is when practical cultural knowledge comes in. Our mothers and other female relatives share their knowledge of roasting and drying corn. This kind of knowledge, when passed down to younger woman, gives them such a sense of empowerment and pride.

With climate change, our growing seasons have shifted even in my lifetime. So to see young families work their fields, the same fields their grandparents cultivated, is a sign of more Pueblo people returning to traditional ways of living.

Food growing helps strengthen familial and community bonds. Of course it's easier to buy a bag of frozen corn at Walmart, but harvested corn made from a tiny seed, irrigated, and nurtured into maturity… there is a deep-seated connection to earth. These young women who have chosen to cultivate a connection to the land are having a unique and rich experience of growing food for their families.

Blessed Beings

Traditionally Kha'p'o farmers moved to the fields to watch over their crops. Whole families camped, safeguarding their fields from hungry animals. Kha'p'o depended on one another. Working together in order to survive was key to our Pueblo worldview, including our prayers and songs that are influenced by seasons and the life cycles of the land. All of this connects us to our cosmos.

When the Spaniards arrived on Pueblo land, one of their objectives was to dismantle Pueblo religion. Priests often went into ceremonial kivas and destroyed sacred objects. This forced Kha'p'o to abandon their religious sanctuaries and find a safe places to gather for ceremony. They gathered near the fields below Kha'p'o Owenge.

Over the centuries, colonization has shifted Pueblo culture. We have young people relocating for school and work, moving away from a more agrarian lifestyle and cultural value systems. That's why our ceremonies are so important. Ceremonies give younger Kha'p'o *towa* the gift of reconnecting to the Pueblo worldview. Those Kha'p'o who continue to live at home, we are strengthened by our ceremonies, the land, and our cultural responsibilities.

During these ceremonies, all of us, whether we dance or prepare food, are mindful that we are all spiritual vessels. I see and feel respect and renewal on those important days. It is powerful to dance in a line with other community members and family, collectively honoring a season or harvest. We lift our feet together in acknowledgment of what we know and have as Kha'p'o towa.

Our prayer is that we carry that strength from ceremony even in hard times. It gives me great joy to see younger generations return to the village to celebrate and renew cultural connections. I see our ceremonies as a metaphoric seed planted in the fertile ground of new generations.

Reviving Tradition

I ask for courage, patience, and kindness when I start my day. Every morning I spend time thinking of my good fortune in health and well-being. In this reflection, I'm continually reminded of my responsibilities as a human being. I think of ways to add to my community. I take the time to engage with young people as well as other tribal members. I want to be a person who listens carefully. I'm mindful that people need to feel respected, especially children. I'm heartened to know our Pueblo community stresses the idea of *ah giin*—Kha'p'o for "respect," in ceremony as well as everyday life.

I am a modern-day elder. I approach and model cultural and community values as best as I can. I believe that our sense of culture can be articulated in many ways: ceremony, renewal of language, kindness. Those articulations of culture leave an imprint for new generations of Indigenous peoples.

My daughter, Eliza, has been actively gardening and planting for some time now. Every year she and her husband grow food in my brother's field. Last season the field produced so much corn, the family spent several weekends gathering and processing the harvest.

I witnessed my older sisters planting a cultural seed by passing on traditional ways of preserving food. My eldest sister, Louisa, who is close to ninety years old, offered her *bunte* for steaming corn. The outdoor adobe oven is heated with quick-burning cedar, and ashes swept out and mopped to create steam for the corn sealed in the oven overnight. Several of Eliza's aunties who also had corn to steam gathered at Louisa's house. Early the next day we opened up the oven to steamed corn. We braided the husks together and, after Louisa's inspection, hung the corn out to dry. We stood back against the adobe wall with our coffee, and visited as the sun climbed over the mountains. Louisa sat near Eliza, and patted her niece's knee with approval as if to say, "You did good." A seemingly ordinary moment, but powerful for Eliza that her auntie acknowledged a season of hard work. Later that morning we baked twenty loaves of bread in the same bunte. Everyone went home with fresh bread and corn for winter soups. It was a memorable morning because women relatives of all ages gathered to experience an articulation of cultural knowledge.

ROSE

My mother, Rose Naranjo, grew up on Kha'p'o tribal land. Like other Pueblo children born in the early 1900s, she was orphaned at an early age. Despite her challenges, my mother raised nine children successfully and she did it with a third-grade education. My mother helped with the family income by making and selling pottery to tourists coming into the village during the summer. She lived through hard times by being resourceful, and because of that we were taught never to waste food or anything else for that matter.

Rose grew up in a large extended family that lived a more agrarian lifestyle. As a child she was raised to survive and to work with her environment, gathering and preserving food for the winter. My mother's survival mechanism was to gather—from wood on the side of the road to her later years when she'd gather up her Green Stamps books and trade them in for dishtowels. Rose modeled a strong will and sense of independence, insisting this trait be taken up by her children, especially her daughters.

Rose Naranjo making a vessel out of clay, circa 1980

My parents were pragmatists. They understood that navigating the dominant culture required Western education, especially if you were a woman. Consequently, all my sisters and brothers have college degrees and have worked in either Native education or in the arts.

Rose was a small, brown woman with a mountain of strength behind her. She believed that our ancestors pushed her forward in everything she did. This was her anchor. Rose was not Western educated. Her knowledge came from a life steeped in Pueblo culture.

In my childhood home, my mother's domain was the kitchen. She often cooked three times a day for her many children and visitors to our home. We shared our food with non-family members who were always welcomed at the table, a Pueblo characteristic that taught us to share with others. Sometimes, after the food had been served and the dishes washed, Rose would take a moment to sit in the back room of the house where she'd make pottery. I understood these precious moments as a time of reconnecting with herself. She moved through her day in fluid motion—from cooking to creating with clay, she modeled an understanding of her place and responsibility to herself and her family. That seamless flow was her foundation, and influenced how we conducted ourselves as Pueblo people.

A Road Made of Glitter

I was immersed in Pueblo pottery making as a child. Because of my father's work, we lived near Taos Pueblo. Our people mine micaceous clay in those mountains, and that's where my mother began working with it. The mica flecks in this clay contain minerals like lithium and magnesium. Around the 1700s, settlers to the Southwest used mica slabs for windows. When mica flecks are ground to a powder, it produces coarse but strong clay that has a brilliant sparkle. This clay area near Taos Pueblo may have been one of my mother's most favorite places in the whole world. Every time we gathered clay at this place a knowing came over her that translated into joy. This was true especially after a rain when the mountain road leading to the clay pit was like a glittering carpet.

The prayers we say before gathering clay acknowledge Nun Chu Kweejo—Clay Mother—and the relationship between the earth and humans. Cultural knowledge as precious as the clay itself formed through prayers and hard work. I incorporate that same value to land sites where I've created public art. No matter where I go or what I do, the thought of where the road glitters anchors my spiritual and creative knowing. There is also practical knowledge in clay work. Seasonal considerations inform clay gathering and processing. All these things have empowered me in other aspects of my life. The true gift from Nun Chu Kweejo is a worldview rooted in ancient beliefs that are sustainable, especially now.

My mother, father, and other elders passed on their knowledge of clay work to me. Role models like Virginia Romero from Taos Pueblo showed my mother and I where to collect micaceous clay. Virginia was known for her utilitarian vessels. One seemingly ordinary day, I saw Virginia gathering clay and emptying it into an old pillowcase. I watched this tiny woman slung the heavy pillowcase onto her back and traversed a steep incline in moccasins she'd sewn the winter before.

All I knew was that I wanted to be Virginia. I wanted to be able to carry clay on my back, too. Virginia modeled what it's like to be a strong woman. I carry that image of her with me when I need to be strong.

After a pit firing, my mother would bundle up her finished pottery and walk into town to sell her work at a local curio shop. On the walk into town I'd notice a change in my mom's demeanor. Rose was preparing herself for the entry into the unfamiliar territory of commerce. She was no longer a matriarch, a respected elder; now she was a brown woman selling her craft to a White man.

The curio shop owner would pick up my mother's vessel and flick his fingers against the bowl's surface to determine how well it was fired. The owner always found flaws with the vessels, which justified his wholesale price. Rose never challenged him; she knew whatever money she made from her work would feed her children. That was the bottom line. After our business was done, we'd leave the curio shop for the quiet walk home. The commodification of culture I witnessed as a child provided lessons for how to maintain my creative integrity.

I still travel on high mountain roads looking for clay. Like my mother, I find great joy in a road made of glitter.

AN ARTIST'S SELF-DETERMINATION

When I started really making art in my early twenties, I had just graduated from college with a social science degree. My first job was at a local social welfare office. Across from my desk there was a huge industrial looking clock that marked every second of the day—tick...tick...tick. On my very first day that clock convinced me I was not suited for office work.

I'm the youngest of eight accomplished brothers and sisters. One day I went to visit my sister Jody Folwell, who is renowned for her contemporary Pueblo pottery. She took one look at me and must have recognized my search for purpose. As we sat in Jody's kitchen, without saying a word she handed me a ball of clay. At that moment I felt like I'd come home. That's how I started creating. I started making small figures and vessels out of clay. And, like my mother, when the clay forms were done, I sold them to tourists at the plaza in Santa Fe, New Mexico.

As I sat on a blanket with other Native artisans, selling to tourists walking by, I continued my questions about earning a living through art. Since my work did not look "traditional," it was suggested that in order to become a successful Pueblo potter, my work needed to look like it was made by an Indian. To deviate from what tourists recognized as "Indian made" would mean I would sell less. Whatever I was making with Pueblo clays expressed my experience as a contemporary Native woman, mother, and human being, and I knew I was not going to deny my creative expression.

In retrospect, selling on the plaza helped me to realize just how important guarding my creative integrity was. There have been these moments, from digging clay to creating, where I'm learning about myself and my place in the world. I consider this a gift. I learned that my success was not determined by how much and whom I sold my work to but what I did with the gift that was passed down to me. This changed my creative trajectory and the way I negotiate the business end of my work.

Making the choice to hold onto my creative integrity empowered me. I began to experiment with new mediums that helped in articulating cultural and environmental issues that were of concern to me. There is a Tewa thought: My purpose is to seek life.

Expressions of Sacred Creativity

Mud Woman is a book of poetry I wrote several years ago. The book speaks to my relationship to clay, family, land, and culture. These relationships are shaped by seemingly ordinary moments like Virginia Romero and my mother gathering clay nuggets high above Taos Pueblo. In *Mud Woman*, I went about gathering *my* memories, like the day I was profoundly struck by an adventure with my father.

"I am a work in progress continually coiling myself with the hope of becoming a whole vessel."

While I was in college, I went for a weekend visit to my parents. I saw my father standing near his truck, looking out toward the barrancas. He was looking for *shu neh*, a grout-like volcanic ash used in pottery to make it stronger. My father nodded toward his truck, I nodded back and got into the passenger's seat. We drove several miles from the village where my father spotted shu neh deposits. It did not surprise me one bit that he found shu neh hidden above a dry ravine in the middle of nowhere. My father knew the land he was born from. Gathering materials like shu neh and wood for firing pottery was not a chore but his anchor.

That spiritual relationship to land sustained my father many years later when illness confined him to a wheelchair. The memories of family, land, and culture that shaped my father's life were still his anchor.

From the little things that are seemingly ordinary events to the largeness of life, I was taught by my relationship to hold these moments sacred because, like shu neh, that makes me stronger. I am a work in progress continually coiling myself with the hope of becoming a whole vessel.

Respect

Ah giin—respect—is important in our little community. Ah giin for land, for culture, for the songs, for ceremonies, for the food we eat, the corn we harvest. Traditional values like respect are integrated into our daily life. Most importantly, these value systems help us in our contemporary Pueblo experience. It's important for our children to know ah giin for themselves because healing from the trauma of colonization will be lifelong. The resources to heal and find resilience comes from our elders, who have the knowledge and tools to help us on our life's journey.

The Earth Is a Stabilizing Force

Several years ago I went to our pueblo's clay pit near the foothills of tribal land. Clay gathering is hard work for one person, so I took frequent breaks. During one of my breaks, I walked a short distance and stood atop a small hill. Looking into a narrow canyon I saw a river of trash—couches, metal, plastic, and everything in between inching toward the clay pit. I stood in disbelief. The visual juxtaposition of the sacred clay pit and the dump was stark and disturbing for me.

The shock turned into curiosity. Walking toward the dump I was compelled to take a closer look. Before I knew it, I had collected a truckload of discarded materials from the dump. I emptied it in my studio and spent a year deconstructing the materials as well as my own attitudes about thoughtless consuming and discarding. Without any creative plan or lofty intentions, I began making art from the materials I gathered. I also began learning about the effects of mass consumption and waste on our environment.

The people I come from rarely wasted any of their resources. My mother was influential that way. Whenever my father and older brothers hunted meat for the family, my mother used every bit of the animal. We were taught that the best way to honor whatever animal came to us was by not wasting any part it. During the Great Depression, Pueblo people repurposed discarded 78 RPM records and old car battery casings to make jewelry. Knowing this history of Pueblo innovation and creativity inspired me to look at this endless supply of discard as a resource. I created large totems from metal fencing, wrapping them with plastic bags from Walmart.

The totems were ten feet high and kinetic. Because of their height, whenever they moved, they'd fall over. To resolve this dilemma, I created stabilizing clay balls for the bottom of each totem. My thinking was, No matter what we as humans do to this earth, the earth is and will remain a stabilizing force.

I started sharing what I was learning about repurposing discarded materials with children in Kha'p'o Owenge and beyond. The Kha'p'o kids I worked with learned about *khaa heh gehs* (traditional Pueblo trash mounds) and the way their ancestors approached repurposing materials.

I want my art to bring attention to cultural and environmental issues that each generation of Pueblo people will face in their lifetimes.

IDENTITY STARTS VERY EARLY

Healing myself of the broken parts that have caused distress is something I've learned from Kha'p'o culture. In turn I've tried to model this to newer generations in my community.

My daughter Eliza is an art teacher at the Kha'p'o elementary school. It's a small school in our community with the intentions of creating a Pueblo-based learning experience for our children. Kha'p'o Owenge is located near the Rio Grande. It's beautiful country. Ironically, there is a busy four-lane road that cuts through the community. For me, that road symbolizes outside social and economic influences that our contemporary Pueblo deals with on a daily basis. Kha'p'o children deal with those outside influences as they navigate what it means to be a Pueblo person today.

Eliza asked that I participate in a yearlong art project at the school entitled *Our Owenge* (our village). *Our Owenge* was an art installation using organic materials to recreate a mini village that students imagined and built as a community. Students constructed the village with small adobe bricks they made themselves. The students were asked to think about what community meant to them. Traditional Pueblo building methods were explored, and elders came to speak about their experiences building and plastering mud homes. Students also learned that other cultures around the world built mud homes.

Our Owenge was made over several months with the children working together. It really was rewarding to witness so many children completely engaged in experiential learning. Tewa was spoken throughout the process. The students channeled cultural information with their imagination to build their idea of community, from a structure they called Tea House to a fortress named Prison With Wings. Some students chose to paint their structures with red clay slip used in Pueblo pottery making. There were Pueblo connections continually guiding the project.

I was honored to be a part of a community collaboration between students and elders that resulted in an art piece and a video. My son Zak and some of the students filmed interviews for the *Our Owenge* video. *Our Owenge* is a unique art project that affirms the sustainability of cultural knowledge.

Eliza took a picture of the fourth-grade boys who made the Prison With Wings. They posed in front of their creation, arms locked around one another. The boys looked empowered, proud, and confident. My hope is that *Our Owenge* planted seeds of possibility that last a lifetime as these students become the next generation of community leaders and educators.

Navi Whageh

I built a studio out of mud several years ago. I worked on my family home when I was in my thirties and had forgotten how labor intensive any kind of construction is, especially when done alone. I needed a place to store my materials and tools. I needed a place where my imagination could be housed and nurtured. Little by little the studio is taking shape and has already become a sanctuary for me. With the help of many people the studio is evolving into a place where creative ideas are realized, where community projects are temporarily housed, and elders have come to tell their stories.

Navi Whageh is my spiritual center. When I was naming my studio, I was thinking how my spiritual well-being has been realized through my work. I view my studio as a sacred place where I feel safe and nurtured to explore my creativity. In the future I hope my daughter Eliza and others will use this space to find their own center place.

*"When one heals, the family heals,
the community heals,
and the nations heal."*

JAN KAHEHTI:IO LONGBOAT

**Kanien'kehá:ka – Six Nations of the
Grand River**

JAN KAHEHTI:IO LONGBOAT is a healer and elder with many decades of spiritual leadership among Native peoples. Kahehti:io is a knowledge keeper, educator, writer, herbalist, cultural advocate, and visionary. Having dedicated her life to the dissemination and learning of Indigenous language and culture, this treasured elder shares her knowledge of Mother Earth traditions through storytelling, fasting, dreams, visions, and profound use of plant medicines. Kahehti:io's lifelong focus is to enhance the self-worth and power of Indigenous women, sharing understandings of women's roles and relationships, messaging in the Haudenosaunee wampum belts, approaches to leadership, environmental change, and the important knowledge that her original language carries for embodying the important values for life.

Kahehti:io represents that our ancestors left us a great legacy of Indigenous knowledge with which we can carry our spiritual, physical, mental, and emotional medicine bundles. Her ten-year program, Idawadadi, won the Aboriginal Healing Foundation's best practices award. The work evolved into an outgrowth project called Dotah's House, to help Indigenous women survivors heal from abuse they suffered at Canada's residential schools.

Kahehti:io inherited cultural skills and a deep sense of peace from her grandmother and other women elders. Through her teaching and gatherings at health centers, universities, and her Earth Healing Herb Garden and Retreat Centre at Six Nations, Kahehti:io guides Indigenous individuals and families back onto a path to peace.

Kahehti:io received an honorary doctorate of law from the University of Guelph in 2011.

Matriline Is our Guiding Principle

Following our mother's line is the guiding principle in our culture. Thus we are born into our mother's clan. I am from the Haudenosaunee Confederacy. I am Kanien'kehá:ka (Mohawk) and from the A'no:wara (Turtle) Clan.

Since 1784, my family has made its home on the Haldimand Tract of our reserve, Six Nations of the Grand River, near Brantford, Ontario. Our ancestral roots come from the Mohawk villages in the Mohawk Valley, what is now known as New York state.

My father comes from the Cayuga people. My great-grandmother Caroline Elizabeth Thomas carried a Turtle Clan title of the Kanien'kehá:ka people. She held the duty of choosing one of the chiefs, under the title of Tekarihoken.[1]

My great-grandmother birthed five girls and three boys. My grandmother Mary Jane Thomas was the eldest. Mary Jane Katsi'tsiahkwa Thomas birthed three girls and three boys, my mother

---

[1] Lead Turtle Clan title. In Mohawk, it means "His matters are split." He carries one mind of peace and one of war.

Vera Katsitsionni being the eldest. My mother birthed twelve children; eight girls and two boys survived. I birthed seven children; three girls and one boy survived. I have thirteen grandchildren and six great-grandchildren.

My grandmother lived a simple, cultured life on the Haldimand Tract of the Grand River. I cannot remember anything that she could not do. It seemed she was able to accomplish everything she set out to do. I listened, watched, and learned how she conducted her life. Her welcoming behavior I never forgot. She received many visitors; some came to visit and some came for medicine. I now reflect back to the many things I learned from my grandma. Her love of Mother Earth became deeply embedded in my body and she has remained my teacher to this day.

Grand River, Six Nations Reservation

Grandma's relationship to the land included her Kanien'kehá:ka language, with which she addressed all life, every day. She spoke to the trees; she thanked the water. She thanked the fire; she thanked the sun and moon. Understanding her cosmology, she interacted with the medicine plants. Grandma carried the knowledge of birth and assisted with the passing in death. Her evenings sitting by the woodstove, smoking her pipe, telling stories, the feeling of peace, I will never forget. It lives in me.

INDIGENEITY OF MY GARDENS

I grew up here at Six Nations. I have lived five generations here. When I was growing up, everyone had a garden and everybody ate off the land. It was just a way of life for my family and all of my relatives that everybody naturally grew up gardening. Truly, it was living off the land.

My grandmother—my mother's mother—inspired me to work with medicines. She worked with medicines for many years, never calling herself a medicine woman but having a lot of knowledge of the plants. I spent a lot of time with her as a child, listening to her stories and observing as people came to her house. It seemed that when my grandma talked about food and when she talked about medicine, she talked about life. She put this bit of mystery to life that appealed to me. That was her way, the way of the elders, to keep us interested in whatever she wanted to teach.

I became so passionate about medicine and food. Coming from a big family with a lot of relatives, it's always been our way to make sure people are not hungry, make sure they feel good. We always feel good through food and medicine. That is one of our ways of making sure people have balance in their life. Naturally, it became my passion to garden. I love having my hands in Mother Earth, feeling her energy. It's an unquestionably Indigenous way of life.

A New Awareness

I spent a lot of time with my *tota*, my mother's mother. I watched her as people came by lantern in the middle of the night, wanting certain medicines. She had baskets of them hanging on her ceiling in her little house and knew exactly which one to use. I got to be seven years old and one day she said to me, "You're old enough now. It's time to help me." She was getting old at that time. "First of all," she said, "you have to prepare yourself for what you're going to do."

At my age, I didn't really understand. She told me to go in the bush and sit by the water, which was almost like a swamp. She had cleared all around this water; it was really beautiful. I went and sat there. Looking back, I thought it was a long time but it might have been only a minute or so. She asked me what I saw. I saw nothing. "Then go back," she said.

I went back a second, third, fourth time. Then, I looked in the water and I saw my reflection, as a woman, as a human being. It was a transformation for me that day. It brought me into the now. I began to be very aware of what was going on around me, the energy and environment. It scared me because I had never had that kind of awareness of myself before. I started to cry and ran back to the house. I told Grandma what happened. She laughed, and said, "That's what I wanted to hear! You learned about you. Now you can come to the medicines and start learning about them. Now you can help me."

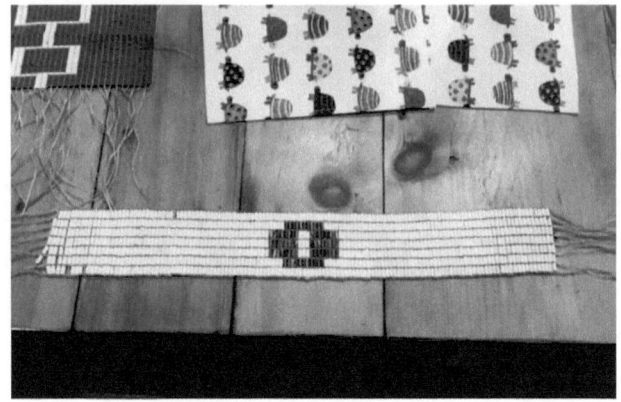

Haudenosaunee wampum belt

Fill up Your Medicine Bundle

The old people said that when you come into this life from the spirit world, you bring a medicine bundle with you. It's up to you to fill it up. They wouldn't say what was supposed to go in it, just that when you're ready, it will come.

I grew up wondering where this was going to come from, where I was going to get what I needed. As I grew, I learned how we fill our medicine bundle. One of the things we have to have is patience. Sure enough, it has come. My bundle is pretty big now, and all of it just came to me.

What goes in your medicine bundle is up to you. The old people said you need to put at least four medicines in there: a medicine that can help build your immune system, a medicine for those that may be grieving, a medicine for birthing. Those are the most common. They said to put four dances in your bundle, so when someone's spirits are down, you can dance. Learn four songs. Put that sound and vibration into your bundle: a traveling song, a morning song, an opening song. Stories are how we carried on with our knowledge. Put four dreams into your bundle. Pay attention to your dreams; they always tell the truth. Those Indigenous tools you keep adding to your bundles.

In every Native community where I've traveled, I have found that the folks know their medicine people. They're not as plentiful as they used to be, but most of our First Nations still have people who know about the medicines. There is a whole belief system based on reciprocity. Approaching a medicine person involves a protocol of giving and receiving. Tobacco is offered to the plant. Medicines are not sold, they're exchanged. Sonkwaiatison, the Creator, is acknowledged for the medicines we've been given to help us through life.

Early Education

Tota is a Mohawk word that refers to male and female elders. I had the privilege of sitting at the knees of totas all my life. I listened to what they had to say and I never questioned it. I assisted them with whatever they were doing. They never asked for help; they expected it. So I helped pick medicines, harvest the garden, pick mushrooms, made bread. I learned through my experience helping our totas.

When I was growing up, we started school when we were seven. It was a good time to begin my formal education. I went to a one-room school with one teacher for eight grades. There was no such thing as kindergarten or pre-K.

When I look back to my early years, a lot of my experience of our family life was in the longhouse, because we were Longhouse people. In earlier times, there were as many as thirty families in a longhouse. So that's the way this one-room school was—many families. I really like that way of learning. Reinforcement is the way our people have always learned. In first grade I heard all the other work up to eighth grade. By eighth grade I had heard it eight times, so it was a breeze to get through our work.

It seems like that's what was happening in the longhouse.[2] I really like that situation. I was really fortunate that it happened. Our community grew up together. It's not that way today back home. They've amalgamated the community schools into three large schools. It divided the community, which is not a good thing.

Our Way of Life

My dad was a great hunter and fisherman. My brothers are hunters. My grandma worked with medicines. She never called herself a medicine woman; neither do I. But she had the knowledge to use the plant medicines. She lived a mile down the road from where I grew up. Now I live in the same house where she lived when I was growing up.

---

2 *Longhouse* refers to the symbolic and actual space that centers the spiritual governance tradition of Haudenosaunee people.

The whole community grew up this same way, living off the land. Not everybody wanted to do the same thing. My choice was to learn about the environment, to learn about land. My dad would go outside and look up into the Sky World. The old people really knew and understood the Sky World. He'd say, you kids better get ready for the rain, it's coming. A beautiful night full of bright stars, and he'd tell us to get the rain barrels ready. We would think, What's he looking at? Sure enough, it would rain that night. Finally, when I was about fifteen, I asked him, "How do you know it's going to rain? What are looking at up there?"

"I'm looking at our grandmother, the moon," he said. "She's holding the water, and she's gonna dump it out tonight." And sure enough, that's what happened. If you watch the moon cycle, the moon is tilted a certain way, it'll dump the water out that night. He was never wrong, and it still happens that way.

Our old people understood weather. At harvest time, Dad would study this hickory nut. Its shell has four parts. If you remove the shell and the covering is thick, we're going to have a cold winter. If it's thin, a mild winter. Nature is never wrong. It knows what to do. The old people call that the Original Instructions. The environment has Original Instructions, and they come from the Creator, Sonkwaiatison. As a child I found that magical. I wondered how we knew all this, and without any formal instruction.

Today that is called Indigenous Knowledge. I just thought it was a way of life. This is Indigenous science of a civilization. We're more than a culture. We are a civilization. We have everything that any other world civilization has today.

My grandmother would say, "What you need to do is learn the language of the universe." I wondered what it was. As years went by, I learned the language of the universe.

Connection of Life Sustainers

We are in the throes of our healing time. The people are coming back to our foods, to living our ways again. It makes me happy when our women come together and sing those seed songs and harvest songs. We're harvesting our food and saving our seeds again. It's important that the women lead. When I was growing up, we had many seed savers. I was taught that the seeds and the food are the responsibility of the woman as nurturer and life giver.

In our Haudenosaunee culture, we talk about the sustainers of life that we call the three sisters: beans, corn, and squash. When we talk about those medicines, we note their vines because they are meaningful to us. The very ways the plants are, teach us that we're also connected by a vine. We are born with our umbilical cord that connects us to our mother, just like that plant comes from their umbilical cord from the earth. We keep that connection because it feeds us, it keeps us alive.

The corn is central. I became so fascinated with this particular corn. It's the old Iroquoian corn, the *onkwehonwe* corn.[3] It has eight rows, where the other corns have lots of rows. This is the old, Indigenous seed that's not hybridized. We make corn soup out of this. We are going to have to come back to this seed. We have to be very conscious of our food and medicines through seed saving. We have many species of beans. I alone save approximately twenty-three species of beans.

We still have all of the foods, all of the medicines—everything we need to sustain ourselves. There's nothing missing. The ceremonies, all the songs…we still have everything. This is what I think we need to bring back into our lives. We need to put into practice our way of life. Since the beginning of time we've known it's been good. There is no doubt that our organic sustenance is still with us.

The sustenance of our whole being is connected to the earth. Indigenous peoples are connected through languages, through

---

3 *Onkwehonwe* is a Mohawk word meaning "the real or original people."

tradition, through everything with Mother Earth. In our Mohawk birth stories, we can see that picture of that connection of the vines and of our own umbilical cords. I am always in awe, because that is so beautiful.

Our Culture Is in the Language

Years ago, when I returned to more fully learning our Mohawk language, I was fascinated with how and what the language tells us. When we understand an Indigenous language, the language connects us to the earth. A Native language will always remind us how we are totally connected to the earth throughout our life.

I spent eighteen years searching and relearning our sacred language. Relearning Kanien'keha has deepened my understanding of the relationship of the universe. I now understand the depth of our cultural expression. I learned the concept of root words and their deep connections to the circle of life. *Tekaneren* is our word for the concept of the circle. It ties and braids all our words, actions, expressions, purposes, and stages of life together. Just learning this one word pushed my spirit back to the beginning of my life's work and showed me that words and action create leadership.

> *"A Native language will always remind us how we are totally connected to the earth."*

All of my family—my mom and dad, aunties, grandma and grandpa—were fluent Mohawk speakers. I heard the language all my life. It was talked all around us, but it was never spoken to us. My dad had been in residential school. Because of the abuse he experienced there, he wouldn't teach us the language. He told us, "I don't want you to be abused for speaking the language, like I was." That was one of my greatest disappointments, not learning our language from my dad.

The old people thought in Mohawk, but taught us in English. They taught us the concepts within the language. It was for our survival. They would always say, "Your culture is in the language." As I got older, I wondered about this instruction. I wanted to find out what they meant. So I went back to Mohawk Valley, our original homelands, for an immersion course. I found the elders were absolutely right: The culture *is* in the language.

A Different Road

I grew up in an environment that was much different than today. There weren't the diseases that we experience today. I think it was because we lived a better life. Everyone on reserve had a garden, lived off the land, and ate good food. The water was clear, unpolluted. The air was much better. Today it's almost an epidemic of diabetes, of cancer, of every kind of disease. I can attest to that because I've seen the difference.

I remember an old woman, Kanon'shirétha. I don't even know her English name—all the old people used their Indian names. Someone asked her when she was 104 what she credited for living so long. "I smoked my pipe every day but I never inhaled," she said. "That was to keep me calm and at peace. I've worked hard. I ate good food." Thinking about her words now, that's exactly the difference. People today don't work their bodies hard, and we don't eat good food.

I realized there is a real key to using our medicines to purify our blood and cleanse our bodies. The old people would purify their blood in spring and fall. In late winter, the thunder beings come to wake up the trees. The first tree to wake up is maple, *wahta*. It gives sap, which purifies the blood, detoxifies the body of poisons. In the winter we drink that medicine again, to make sure we don't get sick.

We need to get back to purification, detoxification, cleansing ways. We did that through fasting and hot medicine baths, or sweat lodges. We are eating bad food, we're not breathing good air, or drinking good water. Life is so much more stressful today. Our young people don't get out and play outside as much. They're so involved in technology. They don't take the time to sit and listen to our old people anymore. We've taken a different road now; we've veered off from what it used to be. I don't think this new road has been very healthy.

Gardens and Wild Game

I've been privileged these past forty years to assist people, especially mothers and daughters, with relearning our traditional food ways—how to garden, save seeds, harvest, and preserve. All of which is easy, once you know how. My mother canned probably one thousand jars of food a year. I know that because I washed the jars! Growing up in our big family, we always had a lot of food. She looked after other people as well and we shared our harvest.

Some of that is happening today. I can see us getting back to having good food again. People are growing more gardens and learning how to preserve their foods, whether it's drying or canning. The hunters bring wild meat home. Some days when I come home, there'll be a bag at my door waiting for me, which is really nice of them, to share their hunt. I've learned to take that buffalo, venison, or moose and make good stews.

The old people used to say your food is also your medicine. It doctors you. I believe that because it's so full of vitamins and minerals. As we begin to teach our little ones again, we will bring back that old way, that good way of eating well and keeping ourselves in balance.

Cycles of Nourishment

As Indigenous people, we follow the cycles of the earth. Our foods and medicines came in cyclical moments. The old people used to say that there's a process to eating. When you get up in the morning, you eat the foods that are closest to the Creator, those high bush berries. When the sun is straight above us, you eat the foods that grow above ground. When the sun has walked its path from the east to the west, you eat the foods that grow below ground, the root vegetables. That will last you till the next day. When I studied diet and nutrition, I looked at our foods. Together they are a complete balance of acid and alkaline. Today we're finding that people are too acidic. When our body becomes too acidic, all kinds of bad things happen. We get ulcers, or gout. Our traditional diet was a complete balance.

In the summertime we ate fish and berries, which are full of vitamins and minerals. Today the doctors tell us to eat more wild blueberries because they're high in antioxidants. Antioxidants fight cancer. Well, our people have known that forever. We've always eaten berries, from the time wild strawberries come right to through the fall, when cranberries are used.

The old people would look out at the trees and say, "Come on, you men, it's time to hunt now." When the trees turn yellow it's time to hunt. I used to wonder, What do leaves got to do with hunting? What they knew was that the animals mate in spring and in the summer they raise their little ones. In the fall, they're grown up. Now the hunters can take mother or father. This tells us that we only ate wild meat such as venison, moose, elk, and so forth in the winter.

My mother was an expert at making corn soup. She'd say, "You have to look at the cycle," and say a Mohawk word, *akoserake*. It's a word that one can think means winter, but it really means to eat white foods. Well, our white corn is "white food." A long time ago, we had the potato bean, a big white bean that we used only in our corn soup. We used beaver tail in our corn soup. If you skin a beaver tail, it's pure white meat. So that's what akoserake recalls for us. When it becomes wintertime, we eat those white foods. We never really ate corn soup in the summer because it's heavy and we did not have refrigeration. It's a winter cycle food.

Our ancient language told us what to eat at certain cycles of the year. It's amazing. But when we went to residential schools and we didn't learn our language anymore, we lost much of our knowing how to do things. I believe our people are the most scientific people in this world. Everything in how we lived was good sense and also good science. I've gone back six summers for Mohawk immersion, and I can truly tell you without a doubt, the culture is in the language.

RESIDENTIAL SCHOOLS LEGACY

For a few decades, it wasn't easy to work with medicines in this community. People began to have fewer gardens. They were buying their food instead of growing it. I think a lot was done to discourage our people from our way of life, and to sell us on other ways of living.

There was a period of time back in the 1950s and 1960s, if the RCMP caught you with medicines, you would get arrested.[4] Our medicines went underground. During that time we still practiced medicines, secretly, in our homes. They were never lost; we protected them. We still have all of our medicines and songs today. Everything we have today is because they were protected by the people.

It is true that times had changed. People worked more off reserve. We had more mobility; people got cars and they were able to go into town and it became easier to buy other kinds of food. It bothered me for a time, why we seemed to put our culture aside. As I grew up I realized that the people who went to residential schools, they weren't able to speak the language. They weren't able to be home with their parents to learn what they were supposed to do. Those government policies really affected generations of our people. It's only now that

---
4 The Royal Canadian Mounted Police are the federal and national police service of Canada.

we're healing from that legacy of residential schools and colonization. We're realizing how important and how beautiful our way of life was.

Multigenerational Wounds

I have been aware of residential schools most of my life, because the school is right here in our community. Formally, it was the Mohawk Institute Residential School, but it is known in the community as "the Mush Hole." The school fed our children only oatmeal, or "mush." The children complained because the food constantly had bugs in it. Everyone I've ever known who had gone to residential school said they remembered being so hungry. My dad always made sure we had a lot of food. When my sister asked him why he bought so much food, he became upset and said, "Don't ever think I would let you go hungry!"

I became aware of the residential school legacy, how it impacted us and left scars on our people, particularly Indigenous women.

My father and three older sisters are survivors of the Mush Hole. That history was not discussed much in our family. But as I understood more and more, I sensed the behaviors that all of these survivors had in common. I missed a lot because of that residential school. It was the reason that, even though my parents and my grandmother were fluent Mohawk speakers, my dad would not teach the language to his children. He told us, "I don't want you kids abused like I was for speaking the language." That impacted me a lot. That cut deep into my psyche. I connected language to culture, but I also had to connect it to abuse. That was a double-edged sword, so to speak.

For over twenty years, I have listened, cried, and healed with the Indigenous women survivors of the residential schools. This personal experience has helped to make me more resilient with the time and space needed for ongoing truth, transformation, and reconciliation. It is during this time that our communities seem to have finally awakened to the loss we've suffered from both residential schools and colonization.

> *"For over twenty years, I have listened, cried, and healed with the Indigenous women survivors of the residential schools."*

Two decades ago, I decided to work for our people through Anishnawbe Health in Toronto. It was the first Aboriginal health center in Canada and the first to be approved to incorporate and work with our culture, using government funding to bring our own teachings into healing. I was hired to work there as one of the healers. I was there for almost six years, working with many healers throughout Ontario, listening to their stories and the stories of the women. I listened to the stories of many hundreds of people.

At first, I didn't quite attach their life stories to the residential school experience. They never really told me they went to residential school; they just had these stories of abuse. After listening to hundreds of people tell their stories, the connection became obvious to me that these were all residential school experiences. I realized I was mainly working with survivors of residential schools and listening to their stories of abuse and the loss of their culture and the pain they've suffered because of it.

Many of them wished to turn their life around, but they didn't really understand how, so that began to be my real focus. I could relate to what they were saying because I also felt a similar pain and hurt, not necessarily because of physical or emotional abuse, but the assault on our language. I began to ask the women questions about residential school. They shared with me their thoughts and feelings and what they felt they needed to transform their lives.

These women were from all over Ontario, and they were telling similar stories. Among the themes I was able to pick out was their sense of loss of their language. It was tied to their loss of Indigenous identity. Then, what they did to lessen the pain, which was generally using alcohol, drugs, that sort of thing.

The residential schools created a generation of loneliness. The women were so lonely because they had been taken away from their families, their cousins, and everyone they loved. When they became lonely, feelings of abandonment set in. They felt so abandoned and hurt, like they had nobody. They lost their self-esteem. At times, they didn't think they were worthwhile to even be helped.

I was very grateful for my knowledge of the culture in which I was brought up. I was happy to be able to help them to know that this is what I grew up with, this is what we do, and I was able to relive that with these women.

In 1999, the Canadian government began to recognize that the Native survivors of their residential school system needed real healing. I proposed to Ottawa to work with survivors, and I began a three-year program, which was called Idawadadi.

IDAWADADI

Idawadadi means "let us speak or share our voices." These women survivors had lost their voices. They couldn't really share deeply how they felt, they didn't even want to be part of the singing, which is healing and a strong part of the culture. They couldn't sing. They truly had lost their voices.

So that was the first thing, to help them find their voice again.

In over ten years at Idawadadi (1999–2009), I worked with over three thousand Indigenous women from all over Ontario. As they healed, the women began to ask to direct their own healing. They told me what they felt they needed, which was to bring culture back into their lives, to find out who they are.

I remember distinctly the very first singing workshop I ran. I thought, Well, I'll try that to see if they can find their voices. I had one of our local singers come in to do the workshop. When she asked them to sing some of the Indigenous songs, they had no voice. They absolutely could not elicit a voice. That was quite a shock to me. It was that night, I thought, Okay, we use our voice in many, many different ways. It's not only speaking, it's singing. It's crying. It's laughing. That evening we actually had a crying workshop, and they found their voice through crying.

It was a very, very traumatic experience for them to even hear themselves cry, but that was the beginning. That was the beginning of finding their voices and asking for the cultural knowledge that had been taken away from them.

I had four healing lodges and I would bring in eight people at a time. I did this for almost thirty years. I did fasting ceremonies with many women, making space in lodges and in the woods for them to be with themselves. That was most rewarding, to witness their self-discovery.

I can honestly say that the reconnecting with our own culture was key. When they realized the beauty and the clear teachings of their Indigenous culture, that is essentially what changed their lives. What helped them transform the most was approaching their Indigenous language, participating in the ceremonies and learning how they could protect themselves with what they needed.

Never Give Up

Healing is a process. People don't all proceed at the same level or the same time. It took some longer to regain their self-esteem, to experience their transformation. Those women who have had a really difficult time making change in their life, or didn't get help in good time, when it might have improved their lives: They need it most. That anger and lost self-esteem boils over to their own families, to their children.

Among our people, those who have suffered the most, who are most beaten down, are the ones who suffer that fate as murdered and missing women and girls. They didn't have good opportunities to gain their self-esteem. They got deep into alcohol or drugs.

Around 2012, I started to work in a group of ten Indigenous elder healers who came together from all over Canada to help residential school survivors and families of murdered and missing women. We traveled all over. We went to them, setting up these healing circles. Most of our work was actually counseling. It was assisting them to find themselves to make change.

That's how we started to work in that area, building their self-esteem, which was one of the main roads for change. We couldn't do it all. We worked with a lot of drug and alcohol centers. We made a lot of referrals to sweat lodges, whatever we felt and they felt they needed. We tried to assist them to find that language, whatever they were or wherever they were, that they felt they needed. It was a range of many Indigenous modalities that we have used throughout our work with the impacts of murder and abduction of our women.

The whole family grows. Once parents and caregivers begin to make change, then their children would begin to make change. When a person heals, the family heals, the village heals, and the nations heal. They begin to change their life and teach their own children the beauty of our culture.

My dream is to see the women take their rightful places again as life givers, teachers, singers, gardeners, leaders, and most of all as the centerpost of their homes. It is my greatest honor to share what has been shared with me, over the course of my life. My story bag is your story bag.

The Indigenous knowledge passed down from generation to generation has prepared the women to never give up. The perseverance and resilience required will always remind us of our roles and relationships within the community.

We are reminded by our elders to search for our sacred places and connect to the ancestral knowledge and energy of our women. The past fifty years have led me to protect our sacred lands, search for our sacred sites, and visit them, to go see the corn pounding stones, petroglyphs, thirteen moon trees, sacred medicine sites, the remains of Mohawk villages, water springs, all of it. My philosophy is the same as my Indigenous mentors: Never give up! Listen, observe, and practice.

The last few decades have been a magical learning experience, not only for myself and the hundreds of Indigenous women survivors, but for their communities as well. When one heals, the family heals, the community heals, and the nations heal.

Transforming Our Justice System

When a person works with people, one doesn't discover everything at the same time. I certainly didn't. But as you listen, you start perceiving the deeper meanings.

When the women began to say that the residential schools' treatment was unjust, they were really saying, "We want justice." At some points during their lives when they wanted justice, it was expressed in anger, in hurting other people. Many, through working in our culture and understanding themselves, turned those feelings around and they realized that if they could change their behavior, they could begin to model their behavior to the world, to other people, to families, to their own children, even to the justice system.

That thought came because of their healing. I had to agree. Yes, what the government has done to us is unjust. It was not only the residential schools. It was everything they've done to us. I began to think about the justice system. I thought, How can we change the justice system to respond to us?

In 2014, Six Nations was fortunate to have two Indigenous justices working in Brantford. Justice Edwards took the lead as they began to work on developing an Indigenous justice component for the court system. He spent six years gathering information. He visited with the chiefs and clan mothers. He visited with the women. Justice Edwards gained a lot of community support from Six Nations and New Credit.

That was hard work because the courts just couldn't understand why we wanted an Indigenous justice system. We persisted where we could, and we appealed to our allies in that field. But when Justice Edwards presented his findings to the court, it made such a strong proposal that the ministry felt they had no choice but to do this project. They decided to try it as a pilot project.

Before long, Indigenous Peoples' Court became an intense piece of our court system. It was very strong for the young people, especially in rekindling their identity and their knowledge of what happened to them. Its value became obvious to the people and showed the differences between Western justice and Indigenous restorative justice.

The Western way of justice is definitely a punitive system. We looked at taking that punitive system and turning it around from an Indigenous perspective. That was really the crux of the whole thing. I don't know exactly how many Indigenous Peoples Courts we have, but they're all across Canada now. It is really quite amazing how strong it's become. That is a movement that supports the transformation young people need for health through their own identity. All of these people who were incarcerated, including youth, would say, "I don't know who I am...I don't know nothing about who I am. I want to know who I am."

They pleaded for help. So instead of sending people back to jail, the justice would remand them back to the community, for a length of time that was appropriate to the case. "But here's what I want you to do," the judge said. "I want you to go and take language instruction. I want you to go and talk to the elders. I want you to go and learn through ceremony, whatever they decide for you."

Many of these young people had left the reserve because maybe their grandmother, who was in residential school, never came back home and went to the city, had become colonized, and lost her language. That was why some of them said, "I don't know who I am." Or they might say, "I heard that I belong to Six Nations" or "I belong to New Credit First Nation" or "I belong to whatever, but I don't know what to do. I don't know who my people are." Disconnected from their people and culture, they became disconnected from their own person.

That was why Justice Edwards or, later, Justice Good would give them a chance to reconnect with their community. The look on the faces of these young people when he would say that, the light went up in their eyes, you could see them think, Oh, my gosh, I can go home! I can come home to that place I heard of, where my people live. Often, just that realization, that hope, is a transformation.

This whole effort became strong because of the concept of the Gladue Court reports, which began out west.[5] We have Gladue writers that go and visit these families and ask what led to the behavior that landed them in the justice system. Come to find out, most of the families of these children that were getting in trouble had residential school survivors. There's a real connection between colonization and residential school, and now it's become intergenerational. I couldn't think of very many cases where residential school wasn't the main factor in our people's difficult lives. It was that connection between residential school and colonization that made me feel the need to exercise some influence on developing an Indigenous court.

---

5 A Gladue report is a detailed plan that gives an offender the opportunity to address issues that caused them to be involved in the criminal justice system. It provides a judge with reasonable options for a meaningful sentence that can help the offender be successful and experience healing.

Belonging

One of the main things that the old people talked about is belonging. It's right in the language, belonging to our time and our space. We've got to belong. That's a human need. That's where I usually begin. I bring them home, so to speak, even if it's only to a memory.

I worked with a lady about a year ago. She hadn't come home in about fifty years. She was originally from Six Nations. She asked if I would meet her off the reserve. She couldn't even come to the reserve, she was so hurt. I asked her, "What is the deepest feeling that she would want to change in her life?" She said, "I want to belong. I need to belong to who I am." She remembered when she was little, these grandmothers would put her on their knee and talk to her. She spoke the little bit of Mohawk that she knew. "They would talk to me in the language," she said, "and feed me." She told me, "All I want to do now in my old age is belong."

As time goes on, some of them are afraid because they hadn't been back home in years. I've worked with these people, brought them here to Six Nations and introduced them to their families. In this one case, they could remember some of their relatives. They were so happy when I actually brought them to meet their family. It was incredible. One of the deepest needs that our people have is to know they belong. To know they have a family who cares for them. What a joy. What an excitement!

Even a simple touch from a relative, they would just break down. Finding an old aunt who would say, "Yeah, I remember you as a child. You went away and didn't come back. I know who you are." That was very strong.

Belonging is key. It's important for all of us, to know where we come from. That's why I think identity is so important, because identity is belonging. It's only then that they have come home, they've come back to their people. What a joy that is, as a human being. It's then that memories and other things will come floating back. This one lady said, "I remember my grandma feeding me corn soup." She hadn't had corn soup since she was a little girl. She was able to place herself in time and feel belonging. I think this is the beginning, the beginning of what many people need.

> *"I'm not an activist. That is a Western way of thinking about it and defining who I am."*
>
> Sarah James
> **Neets'aii Gwich'in**

SARAH AGNES JAMES sings a caribou welcome song to educate the world about the Gwich'in way of life. She encourages the people to "learn from each other and go forward for the earth, so we can live." Sarah's life and story are inseparable from the far northern world of Interior Alaska.

Sarah is the formal spokesperson on the Arctic Refuge issue for three Neets'aii Gwich'in tribal governments—the Arctic Village Council, the Venetie Village Council, and the Native Village of Venetie Tribal Government—that own 1.8 million acres at its borders.

In 1988, Gwich'in leaders from across Alaska and Canada gathered their people in Arctic Village when oil interests threatened to invade their region. The elders issued a statement formalizing their opposition to oil development in the Refuge: "The health and productivity of the Porcupine caribou herd, and their availability to Gwich'in communities, and the very future of our People is endangered by proposed oil and gas exploration and development in the calving and post-calving grounds in the Arctic National Wildlife Refuge."

The elders' stand mobilized a movement among their people to find and educate allies who would help them protect the natural environments of their northern world. Sarah and others mounted a campaign against all odds, and have resolutely created formidable and, to date, successful obstacles. During the three decades since, Sarah emerged as one of those advocates who embodies and has come to symbolize her cause.

Sarah grew up living off the land and knows the ways of surviving in the cold north country. She dedicates herself to protecting necessary lifeways, amplifying the voices of her people and beings—especially the caribou. The land is her teacher, her medicine, her sustainer, and her way to the Creator. While a student in San Francisco, she was involved during the occupation of Alcatraz Island by activists from the American Indian Movement. Still, she always emphasizes, "It was not where my activism started. I was born with it."

Inevitably, she has received numerous recognitions and awards, including the Goldman Environmental Prize for 2002. Sarah was inducted in 2009 to the Alaska Women Hall of Fame. She was honored by the Wilderness Society, which awarded her its Robert Marshall Award in 2015. Sarah modestly shrugs off such awards and continues to travel widely, always mobilizing her audiences with empathy for the protection of the Porcupine caribou herd and their calving grounds from oil development and climate catastrophe. Sarah works from her village and remains devoted to passing forward the ancestral values and teachings to younger generations.

I Was Born This Way

I'll start with our traditional way of introducing myself. My name is Sarah James. I am Neets'aii Gwich'in from Arctic Village, Alaska. My mother is Martha James, and her parents were Reverend Albert E. Tritt and Sarah Tritt—caribou people from Arctic Village. My father is Ezias James from Birch Creek, along the Yukon River, and his parents were Agnes James and Birch Creek James—salmon people. And so I'm caribou and salmon people. I am honored to be named after both of my grandmothers—Sarah Agnes.

I'm not an activist. That is a Western way of thinking about it and defining who I am. I don't need to be defined in Western ways. I was born this way. We already know who we are. My way of life is the life I know. It's this way for Indigenous people. My people always operated to survive; our life was all about what life can provide for us. That's what makes us who we are. It's not our choice. It's how God made us.

Struggle for Survival

At this time in my life, I represent my tribe, our sovereign government, as a spokesperson for the struggle to protect the Arctic Refuge from oil exploration and development. We, the Gwich'in people, are struggling for our survival by defending the calving, nursery, and training grounds of our caribou herd. This is at the Arctic National Wildlife Refuge (ANWR), a protected refuge since 1960—and to us, a source of life since time immemorial.

Today our very way of life is threatened by the proposed development of oil and gas in the coastal plain of ANWR. That development is a threat to my tribe, regardless of where we live or what kind of work we do, because it is a threat to the caribou, and the caribou are in our hearts. We believe that we are in the caribou's heart and the caribou is in our hearts, and that's how we've survived together for thousands and thousands of years.

WE ARE CARIBOU PEOPLE

We call ourselves caribou people. A spirit man, *Vasaagihdzak*, which means "a man who travels," or *Ch'iteehawkwaii*, which means "he paddled his way around," visited every animal in creation and corrected their way of living. At the time, most of the animals preyed on humans, but this man told them not to do that. He taught each animal their proper food to eat. "This will be your life from now on," he said.

"The Porcupine caribou herd is my life.
It makes me who I am."

Vasaagihdzak observed and corrected all the animals he visited. When he came to caribou, he stayed with them for a week to observe their way of life. He concluded that the caribou were very well organized and strong. They were clean and healthy. They had their own food and a clean environment. There was nothing he thought they needed to change. And so he went on his journey. I thought that was a pretty special kind of story that I heard about caribou. And like I say, our elders always say that we're in the caribou's heart and the caribou is in our heart, which means that they take care of us and in return, we take care of them. We are proud of who we are, the caribou and us.

The Porcupine caribou herd is my life. It makes me who I am. My people grew up with caribou, depending on them for everything. In return, we also take care of the caribou and the environment so that our caribou are healthy.

We tell stories that are related to our culture and tell of who we are. All our traditional songs and dances are prayers to keep the caribou and environment healthy. We sing caribou songs and dance the caribou dance to keep them healthy and to be proud of who we are in relationship with them. The caribou are food on our tables. Even today, 75 percent of our food comes from hunting and fishing, mainly caribou, moose, Dall sheep, small animals, birds and ducks and fish, and gathering plants and berries. The caribou also provides clothing for us—our boots, mitts, and hats. Wild food is a medicine for us—the animals, tree pitch, and even water are medicine. The caribou provides some of our tools—specifically one long piece of leg bone that is used to scrape the inside of the caribou skin. We use other bones and antlers and even hooves for our arts and crafts. The caribou even provided our original shelter because our tents used to be made of caribou skin. That's how we survived and stayed alive throughout history. The caribou are our way of life.

We Come from Here

We always have been here. We never came from anywhere. We believe that Creator, God, put us here to take care of this part of the world and that's our responsibility. We're here to stay. If we went anywhere, there's a story about those people and where they went, because we have always been here. We were told that we came from here.

We are told that at one point we got overpopulated and it was very difficult to feed so many. We got too many people in one place. People had to make a decision. If we all stay here, we are going to have hard times; there won't be enough.

They said, maybe where the sun sets, maybe that's where there's land of plenty. They had noticed that in the springtime, when the sun come up, that's when plants and animals start coming in and things grow again as it warms again. The sun always sits in the north for us; that's where the sun sits. They thought, That's where we should go because it should be a land of the plenty, wherever the sun sits.

So they left only so many people here. They would lift up the land again, make it abundant. The rest of the people went toward the sun. They came upon the Arctic Ocean. There they left a little bit of people and some stayed. Then they also went east and west across ocean from there, they split up, and some went south. They said that's how we went out into the world.

Some scientists say the whole Ice Age missed our place. I figure that we must have stayed here a long time and over time we overpopulated. The geography shows that the Ice Age never got here, and there is no lava. These mountains are all different and unique. They're not like the kind of land that it is formed by receding ice. We always believed that we came from here. Some say all people came from here. Of course, many people have their own creation stories. So I can't go and say that everybody came from here. But that's our story.

Our people understand what's going on up in the sky. There's a story about the sky and the stars and the moon, and everything about the sky and the weather and the sun, everything up in the sky and the surroundings that we depend on for our life. I kind of neglected listening to my mom about the sky, so I missed out on some of that. But there are a few Gwich'in that know those stories pretty well. One young man told the story recently to a university group and I was so happy that there are people even a bit younger than me who can do that.

We have sun. We know that without sun there won't be any life, and that the stars provide the direction. We have a northern lights story. Our people know where every star is at and at what time and all that kind of knowledge. They respect the sun, by having their caribou skin hut doorways to the east. If you're sitting inside the caribou skin hut there would be sixteen poles, and the largest doorway is to the east, because that's where the sun rises.

Watch the Sky

One direction from the elders is always that everybody my age or older, and even the young those days, are supposed keep an eye and watch what's surrounding them and always watch what's going on in the heavens and surroundings.

If something is too different, then that means bad news. Just like climate change—change in weather, change in what the sun is doing, or what the sky is doing. It might take a while before it brings it, but it is really bad news. It's a threat. They said over time big change will mean bad news.

So I was taught always to be aware of and watch the surrounding. "Make sure you always watch the sky," the elders said. "See if there's anything changed from the normal." That's our instruction that I know from way back and people always told us that.

A Sovereign People

We are part of this land. We believe that the Creator God left us here to take care of this part of the world. We never believed we had come over from the land bridge, and that kind of stuff. We are our own people.

We have a great chief from way, way, way back, the last great chief we can ever remember from a long time ago. He's the chief that we all originated from. He was capable of being chief of a whole people, a whole nation. They say that he wore a silk scarf around his neck. I asked, "Where did he get it from?" "Well," they said, "he earned it. It is his."

We as a people have had trade and a barter system from way back, and we always communicate with our surrounding neighbor peoples. We have neighbors all around. We have our own borderline. We have our own territories. We got Iñupiat Inuit people up to the north; that's our north boundary people. Those are Inuit. Then there's Koyukon over to the east, and over to the west is Cree. All around, different tribes.

We always respect our borders with each other, and always we trade and barter or visit. But if we intrude on their land, they'll tell us right on the spot. If they come over without proper announcement, if anyone sneaks in that way, then that can be bad on the spot, too—even deadly. So we hold strict boundary like that, back and forth on each other. We always did that with respect and honesty and honor.

That's what I say about being a sovereign people.

Mother Teachings

In our ways, as you become a woman, they teach you the history of our tribe and how to do things. There's a long process that they practiced, from a long time ago, preparing a girl to become a woman.

I have many, many teachers. The main one is my mother because I was raised on the land. Being that I'm the last one in the family, I ended up staying at home with her when everybody else was out. So she told me stories, and that's how we learned.

My mom explained to me that the woman is the most important energy. Woman has the strongest power because she bears child, she bears life, and that's the most powerful thing for a human being. Life is the most important instruction and she has to pass on her power. For that reason, she said, woman is very powerful, more than man, but to share our power with man will give him power.

My mom also said that in order for a woman to give a life and have a baby, and to direct that child into the world, she has to have great patience. If she doesn't have that patience, it won't help the child because the mother won't have given her or him power. She has to give the child power to be a human being. In order for a woman to do that, even though she does have the power, she has to learn how to be patient and learn to share.

Becoming a Woman

For becoming a woman, they would start the girl on training as they were born, but when they become a woman, the elders are going to have to help them prepare themselves. In their time of change, they will be isolated for one whole month. During that time, a woman could come and visit and spend time, do things with her, but men could not visit her.

They have this long bonnet; it's like a hat or visor that has you look down to the ground. There are three portions to it. They wear it and they are not to look around for one whole year. Every three months, it gets cut back until there is no bonnet anymore. They cut off a portion, until she doesn't have to wear it anymore. All that is to teach them how to listen and to listen well, with nothing to disturb them, taking their attention and awareness. That's how they learn patience. They get that power, and they have to learn how to use their power in a good way.

I was behind the curtain for about a month. I had to stay home most of the time and be around the house. Many kinds of things I would learn as a young woman. I had to learn how to take care of myself, how to clean myself, how to deal with the monthly cycle. I have to learn how to sew and listen to stories. Different women come by and they tell me a story. Or my friends come and visit me. I don't get to go out late at night. I am not to go to any single man's place. We learned not to sit on a single man's bed or anything like that, for respect.

One thing important in our culture is how to take care of your hair. Our hair is our life. We call it life and it's not something that you ignore. You are supposed to take care of it. We're not supposed to cut it and do stuff like that. We have to take care of it and keep it clean and nice.

I had to be around the house, so I learned how to cook. I learned how to run the house. I would take care of the kids. My mom, me, and my dad, we ended up taking care of my sister because she had a lot of kids and she got sick. Her husband got sick. So much of our time we were tending to the kids and other kids' needs.

All my older brothers and sisters went to boarding school. I was left at home. I could go to school, but I could not go anywhere else. I had to come straight home. We just had a little one-room school for a while. When we finally got a bigger school where there were two rooms: for older and younger.

The boys, too, go through a training, where they get instruction on how to treat women and where they stand as a man. I don't call it a ceremony; it's training. The boys learn how to take care of it all, to live with little water and to take care of their weapons and tools. There are men to teach them what they need to learn.

My mom would tell me that there is a power we have that we give the men, in order for our men to have a strength. She many times told me that I can't take advantage of men because they don't have a strength. That's what she told me: "You walk behind him, give him that power. And he'll feel it. It'll give him a power that helps the family. You should not take advantage of that, but as a woman you are the one that can make your man a better man and a strong man."

Beginnings of Village Life

We were colonized as a people, now for some 150 years. Before that, we were one people. They call us a "band." I don't know why. One people, I say. We were a nomadic people of many families and bands. We moved about with the herd or other food sources, traveled to places for certain seasons and times. Sometimes, one family would spend a winter in one place, or maybe a little patch of people will spend seasons in one place because the harvest was good or whatever reason. And sometimes lots of people settled in one place because they had a good harvest from a caribou fence or something like that.

Arctic Village is one special favorite place because caribou tend to come through there. There is a good creek down here, we call it Vashraii K'oo, a creek with a high bank. That creek is popular because the fish move in the springtime or falltime, and that is where they come out into the river. That's a good place to put fish traps. Our way of life was in movement, what they call "nomadic."

What finally colonized us, I think, was school, when the government said the kids have to go to school. Because then, in order for our kids to go to school, they would have to go to a boarding school or a foster home or be adopted, or they would just be taken. Some of the people had to settle or colonize in one place so they could start a school in order to keep their kids.

They tried to settle where they could survive. They settled here in Arctic Village because they can survive. Caribou tend to pass this through. We have a tree line and many waterways from East Fork of Chandalar River, K'aiieh'chuunjik, that runs into the Yukon River. All this is full of lakes, this valley. If we have nothing else to eat, there would be fish. So that's why we settled there. They did that for Yukon; they did that everywhere.

That's how we got more settled and colonized as a people into village life. For us it turned out to be fifteen settled villages, both Canadian and US. We had seen up close that colonizer mind, so we just tried to keep the villages going, so the kids won't be taken away to boarding schools and so forth. And since we're not the kind of people that stays in one place because we're nomadic people following the caribou, to every corner of our country we went. We were separated by the Canadian-American border for 150 years.

Away from Home

I didn't go to school until I was nine years old. My mom kept me home more and we lived out in the land. When I was thirteen years old and way behind with the schoolwork, I went to boarding school.

The boarding school was Wrangell Institute, in Wrangell, Alaska. You've got to have an eighth-grade level to go onto the other boarding schools in Alaska. I didn't have the eighth-grade level, but they have a vocational school in Chemawa, Oregon, where I did not need to have it, so they sent me there next for boarding school. When I got there, I got tested. I could only read second grade level and I was thirteen. So I started out very late.

> *"It was very difficult to change my picture from being out in the land to a boarding school."*

My first speaking language was Neets'aii Gwich'in. English is my second language. I have no degree but high school, which I got at boarding school. I was one of the oldest ones out of the woods.

It was very difficult to change my picture from being out in the land to a boarding school.

I went a long distance—from Alaska all the way to Salem, Oregon. It was totally different from what I knew out in the land. It was scary. It was a hunger, lonesomeness, and feeling of loss. At that time, I had to work about twenty-four hours every day just to try to understand what they're talking about. The teachers... nobody could understand where I came from. I think most people still don't understand that.

I was lonely for my home, and always hungry. They fed us three meals a day, but it's a different kind of food. As much as we ate, we still were hungry because it's not our food. That's why we were hungry, even though they fed us three square meals. It's just different foods. All it did to us was make us gain weight.

Catching up My Studies

I had to study all the time in order to catch up with students my age and in order to get out of there. If I don't study, I don't get out.

Still, we were lucky to go to Chemawa because there they didn't beat up on kids. They did that in other places, but there's not really a bad story about Chemawa. It was a good system there. We learned a lot; I did, and a lot of my class did. I graduated with about four hundred other students. Most of them are happy they went to Chemawa and they learned a lot and there's hardly any story of bad times.

I didn't understand and still I don't speak English that well. Those were hard ones for me. Some of the kids were right up on pace with Western education, right on that level. They were from families with money. Some of the kids from other places, more southeastern Alaska tribes, they have a lot more money. Those students got all kinds of stuff that we, the ones from up north, did not.

In the north, we don't have money. My mom and dad, they never find eight hours of work a day. They just earn their money as best they can—my dad from carpentry and trapping and whatever he can do. But he brings in food for us. That's how I grew up and they never really had money.

Maybe at school I might get $20 for Christmas, maybe just $10. And sometimes in between I get $5 or $10. I have to work weekends. A whole weekend in my work, I'm lucky if I make $5. That means cheap things; cheap nylons that rip really easily, cheap shoes that fall apart, that kind of stuff. It's really a hardship, because as children, we felt we had to keep up with everyone else, whatever they require. Most of the time we don't have that.

I would go to the school in August and come back in May and then we're home for summer. Because I was behind in school, I stayed for summer school two times, and then I could come home for only two weeks. The last year before my senior year, I stayed for summer to work. This was so I can have my senior rings, gown, yearbook, and stuff like that. I worked hard so I could have my senior year.

Sarah James

Rebirth of Our Gwich'in Nation

Back in the day, when a big problem developed, our people would come together and mingle for a few days and resolve the problem. We let that kind of get-together go sometimes, but our people still carry that for the generations. That's our way.

In 1988, a major disturbance to our nation came up when we were threatened by huge oil companies pushing to open caribou calving grounds in the Arctic National Wildlife Refuge Coastal Plain to oil and gas development. To us, this area is Iizhik Gwats'an Gwandaii Goodlit, Sacred Place where Life Begins. After many years of separations, at that time, people determined that our traditional big gathering was needed. It happened in Arctic Village, June 5–10, 1988. What happened at that one gathering was like a rebirth of our whole nation.

Our way of life was threatened. Even today, all those villages depend on that one Porcupine caribou herd. And that was threatened; its calving and nursery and training grounds were threatened. So that coming together was very deep, like a rebirth of a nation. The elders heard from people, then they took over the meeting and put aside the rest of the agenda. They said, "We'll do it in our way." All the fifteen chiefs got involved and said that this is really good, just like a rebirth. Our nation has come together. The world needs to hear about us, and the only way the world will hear what is happening is if we put it in black and white.

The chiefs separated themselves from the meeting and sat around the camp's fire. They wrote this very clear statement that we live by even today. That was 1988. There we formed the

Gwich'in Steering Committee, a nonprofit organization, to tell the world who we are as a people and why we stand for the great Porcupine caribou herd. Our elders were very, very, very sad and concerned. They were crying. They were singing. They were praying. Gwich'in Steering Committee is founded on spiritual foundation. We have reaffirmed the resolution of the elders every two years.

> *"The only way we can do it is if we can make friends and we have to do it in a good way. Educate the world why we say no to oil."*

We didn't know quite what to do, because nobody knew us. People don't know where our Arctic villages are. They don't know about the Porcupine caribou herd. They don't know Gwich'in. Many people think that everybody up here lives in the igloo and the Eskimos (Inuit) and polar bears and all that. The elders said that we can't do it on our own. The only way we can do it is if we can make friends and we have to do it in a good way. Educate the world why we say no to oil.

Sarah James at Capitol Rally to Defend Arctic Refuge with Representative George Miller, DOI Secretary Bruce Babbitt, 1995

We Know Climate Change

At that gathering in 1988, Norma Kassi, one of our Native sisters in Canada, alerted us. She said, "We're in a great change. Look at the sky. Look at our water. Look at our forest," she said. "Look at us. There's been a change. There's a great change. There's a global warming. There's a climate change."

It is true. We know. Where we are, this used to be the tree line but now that tree line is about a hundred miles north from here. More growth is coming in. Different animals are coming in with it. We never used to have polar bear. But now, with climate change, there are stories about polar bear, how they come this far south looking for food. Also, black bear, who had never been in this country. Woodpecker had never been in this country. When they decide to settle here in Arctic Village, unlike now, we never had a tall birch tree. Now we got few birch trees when cutting wood. So along with the change, new birds and animals come in looking for their home, where they find their food.

At that gathering, we could all agree that Gwich'in thinks different. The birds, the ducks, the fish, the caribou—they are welcome here. We have grouse in our backyard. We have fox in our backyard still today. We have many fish in our lakes and creeks. Caribou passes by the school, across bridge over the creek and the village. We don't hunt around the village or five miles from the village so the caribou and other animals around us feel safe.

The Arctic Village was formed because of that creek. So we call Arctic Village *Vashraįį K'ǫǫ*, a creek with high banks. Back in the nomadic days, this used to be a favorite stopover, and they also stop here to get their fish.

We have been a strong people, because we could live on the land. We are more settled now, but we still live with the land. I remember with my mom back when I was growing up out in the land. We had everything there. And today we've still got everything there. We moved place to place to place. We own very little. But we have dogs that are smart and know us, understand us. We didn't have to tie them up or anything like that. They laid down so we can put their packs on and then we helped them get up.

I remember one night my sister got sick so they had to take her to Fort Yukon. It took two sleds full to do that, over unbroken trail. We had a leader dog named Fox. And with that leader dog, my dad came and went up fifty miles in each direction from where we were. They told Fox in our language where to go, through unbroken trail. He remembered his way and they broke trail back to Fort Yukon with that sled.

Defending Arctic Refuge and Gwich'in Way of Life

Our people accepted the chiefs' 1988 resolution to defend our lands and the Porcupine caribou herd. When they made that decision, our elders said, the only way is to make friends. From then on, we educate the world about who we are, why we say no to oil, in a good way, stay united, no compromise, and gather every two years to do the same resolution. From 1988, we organized as a nonprofit organization to educate the world. We did much good as the Gwich'in Steering Committee, educating the world. We held our own.

Our tribe, Neets'aii Gwich'in, has been here from time immemorial. Our land here, 1.8 million acres of land, is titled "to us from us" from back in 1938 under IRA when our own John Fredson was in leadership.[1] He's the first Athabaskan Indian guy from our region that got a master of arts. I didn't know exactly where Athabaskan come from then, but I knew for an Athabaskan Indian to get a degree, and that he came back to our village, came back to Venetie, that was important.

John Fredson was the one who knows the law changed and talked to his people about how we could apply for the Indian Reorganization Act. That's how we got settled 1.8 million acres of land as the Venetie Indian Reservation.

We've always been exercising our sovereignty rights and governing ourselves. We continue our sovereign right to govern ourselves. We manage the Porcupine caribou, regulating our hunting and fishing.

Happy in Our Traditional Territories

I say, right now is a very happy time with special excitement for us here in Arctic Village because the caribou have arrived from the north.

---

1 John Fredson (1896–1945) was a Neets'aii Gwich'in tribal leader from near Table Mountain in Alaska's Sheenjek River watershed. He is most noted for gaining federal recognition for the Venetie Indian Reservation in 1941, then the largest reservation in Alaska, containing approximately 1.4 million acres.

We're on 1.8 million acres of privately owned tribal land, our Native Village of Venetie Tribal Government land. Our traditional territory is a much bigger area around us where the caribou migrate during the year and where we still hunt and fish and gather from the land. Across the river from Arctic Village is the Arctic National Wildlife Refuge where the caribou come to us from their calving and nursery grounds.

We're so happy that we're going to eat well again because the caribou have come in abundance. Our hunters went out and came back with meat for everyone in the village plus our neighbors, so we all can share. When we look out and see the caribou, our hearts beat fast. We are so excited. This morning I built my fire to warm up my house with wood. I've got caribou meat to cut out in the yard. I just got it last night, and I can't leave it too long, so I have a lot of work to do to make use of every part of the caribou before it spoils.

Most of our people live off the land hunting and fishing. That's our way of life. It's just like a job to us. Our way of life is shared so that everyone can eat: the elders have their meat, single women have their meat. That's what's going on right now—we're dividing and preparing the meat for the village. It's a lot of work, but it's a good feeling to be cheerful and thankful and do it together.

When the caribou don't come near the village, though, it's very hard. Before our contact with the Western world we were nomadic people and traveled place to place where we could gather and harvest caribou and other food. Now we are colonized into village life. Our kids have to go to school and some people have to work.

We're one of the most remote villages in the United States, 110 miles north of the Arctic Circle. Everything we buy—like coffee, or flour, or sugar—has to be flown in. We pay $10 a gallon for gas for our boats, snow machines, and ATVs. That's very expensive, so we really have to share our vehicles with everyone in town. We used to travel by dog team, or walk, or drift down on a skin boat and get back with canoe or walk with dog packs, but now there's an airplane that flies in every day with the mail and other basic supplies. There's no convenience store around the corner, so we're basically out on the land surviving on our own. It's a hard life, but it's a healthy life.

We live in two worlds. We teach our children to respect their elders, go back out on the land, learn our ways, and be proud of who they are. At the same time, we tell them, "Go to college. Get a higher education." We do have K-12 in Arctic Village, and we encourage our young people to get a higher education as well. If we can learn both ways, I think it will be a lot better for our people and all people. To us, it's seventh generation since Western contact. I've been caught in two cultures all my life. My mom didn't have any Western education. I learned more about life growing up and being out on the land with my parents and this meant more to me than Western education. It wasn't easy for my mom; it hasn't been easy for any of us.

Teach the World in a Good Way

We have survived since time immemorial because we govern ourselves as a tribe and the land and protect it. We always have had tribal leadership in protecting our lands. When our nation was at risk from danger in the past we came together. The elders remind us that we must take tribal leadership as we always have in the past. When the elders first asked us to take our story to the world to protect our way of life, it felt like we had no power. Our elders prayed and sang prior to asking us to do this because, although we feared oil and gas development, we also feared the traffic that might follow from the world learning about this last protected wilderness.

They said we should endeavor to teach the world in a good way about why we were saying no to oil and gas development. And we did—with Congress, American people, the world, everybody. We made many, many friends. One homeless man even became one of our best friends because he saw our story on the newspaper he was sleeping on! So we helped educate the world in a good way. We have shown people that this is not only a Neets'aii Gwich'in issue; it's an American issue because it's public land we're protecting.

Sarah James with Secretary of the Interior Sally Jewell, 2016

Sarah James with Senator Hillary Clinton Arctic Refuge Rally, Washington DC, 2013

Although this is an environmental issue for us, it's also a human rights issue. Everyone saw what happened to the buffalo, which were critical to the survival of the Plains Indians. That's why other Indian nations are in solidarity with us through the National Congress of American Indians, the Tanana Chiefs Conference of forty-two tribes in Alaska's Interior, and many individual tribes across the United States. There are many tribal governments coming to join us; it's an issue of tribal sovereignty rights. We have support from the International Indian Treaty Council, the Indigenous Environmental Network, and from people of color and Indigenous leaders in the Environmental Justice Leadership Forum. We also have support for our human rights from churches—first the Methodists, then Episcopalians and many others. The Union for Reform Judaism supports our human rights because they have experienced genocide. We have women's groups speaking for us, because women can relate to the caribou birthplace and post-calving nursery and the need for a clean, quiet, private, and safe place for birthing and raising young and training.

WE'RE GOING TO WIN ONE DAY

Today, I'm representing my tribe, our sovereign governments, as a spokesperson for ANWR. This is my next step, after the work with the Steering Committee. On this issue, we must negotiate sovereign to sovereign.

We're doing government to government consultation, sitting across the table—our tribal governments and the US government—and standing our ground for the Coastal Plain of the Arctic National Wildlife Refuge, the Sacred Place Where Life Begins, Iizhik Gwats'san Gwandaii Goodlit, that sustains us as Neets'aii Gwich'in.

I always like to remind the people of that Gwich'in *niintsyaa* (gathering) in 1988, when the Gwich'in from Canada and the United States came together for the first time in one hundred years to stand up for the Porcupine caribou and our way of life. We all came together in Arctic Village with the fifteen chiefs, fifteen elders, and fifteen youth leaders. At that time, and since, the US government has threatened to allow gas and oil development within the Porcupine caribou birthplace. It came close under the Trump administration, which posed a great threat.[2]

> *"In our hearts, we know we're going to win one day, because it is the right thing to do."*

---

[2] Through the backdoor in the massive tax bill of 2017, Congress removed Arctic National Wildlife Refuge protections from oil and gas leasing and development in the Coastal Plain. The Trump administration rushed the environmental impact statement process and then held an oil and gas lease sale in its final days in January 2021. The lease sale was a fiscal failure; only a few small companies and the state of Alaska bid on leases. President Biden put any lease exploration and development activity on hold on his first day in office. Our Neets'aii Gwich'in tribes have a lawsuit, and the first Native American Secretary of the Interior Deb Haaland has required a new environmental review.

Back then, the public didn't know Gwich'in. They didn't know Athabaskan Indians. They didn't know Arctic Village. They didn't know Arctic National Wildlife Refuge. They thought everybody in Alaska was Eskimo and that we lived in igloos. But today, after thirty years of going out into the world to explain why we say no to oil, they know about us. They know about the Coastal Plain, the birthplace of the Porcupine caribou herd. We made many friends. And repeatedly, loud and clear, across the whole United States, Americans have been with us, and they are still with us and have spoken clearly. This year, the polls say 75 percent of Americans want no gas and oil development of the Coastal Plain, the Porcupine caribou birthplace and nursery of the Arctic National Wildlife Refuge. They clearly want the US Congress to keep the refuge protected.

We believe that the US government needs to recognize rights of permanent protection for the caribou for our people and many life forms.

We need everybody's help because the Arctic National Wildlife Refuge is public-interest land. We can each do something to restore protections from oil and gas and to permanently protect the birthplace and nursery grounds of the Porcupine caribou herd, the sacred place where life begins in the Arctic National Wildlife Refuge.

For us, it's very, very critical and very sad. It is sadness for what could happen to our people and our way of life. But in our hearts, we know we're going to win one day, because it is the right thing to do.

"Our people say the cultural traditions have been sleeping and now we are waking them up!"

Yvonne Dupuis Peterson

Chehalis

YVONNE TOON NEE MU SH DUPUIS PETERSON invites us to "sit beside" each other to learn—the way her mother showed her to live a caring life.

A master weaver from the Hazel Pete family, Yvonne is an enrolled member of the Confederated Tribes of the Chehalis Reservation. Growing up rich in salmon, berries, and much natural bounty, Yvonne was taught to work hard for family, community, and self in the prairie and river lands of her people. Her ancestors are woven into her consciousness and actions, she breathes their same breath, and walks the paths they created for her generations ago. Weaving is the foundation of her cultural understandings. Weaving baskets connects her to the Chehalis natural world, as strands of plants and memories coming together in a beautiful, contained wholeness to carry into the next generation.

Expressing her prayers as poems, Yvonne seeks, in her own words, to transform the past into the future through a prism of caring. She is a political scientist, educator, and intergenerational cultural awakener who weaves together traditional and academic methods at home and at Evergreen State College, where she is a founding member of the Indigenous studies program and where she has taught for the past thirty-six years. In our culture, she likes to remind us, "You don't teach everyone the same weave because then they won't need each other."

Yvonne received bachelor's degrees in elementary education and ethnic studies from Western Washington University, and a master's degree in political science from the University of Arizona. With her husband and teaching partner, Gary Peterson, Yvonne has collaboratively designed and teaches interdisciplinary courses that center Native arts, culture, education, political science, and advocacy to shape the next generation of Indigenous leaders, creators, and agents of change. In recognition of her decades of service to Native students and communities, Yvonne was awarded the Enduring Spirit Award from the Native Action Network in 2015.

Toon Nee Mu Sh

I'm Yvonne Peterson. I'm Chehalis, Nisqually, Potawatomi, Sac, and Fox. I am a Chehalis tribal member. My tribal name is Toon Nee Mu Sh. In our language, my adult name means "my village is sending a person." I had received my certification as a public school teacher, and I was going to the Skokomish village to work with their people. So my elders selected a name that would represent my life's work. They were saying, "We as a people are sending Toon Nee Mu Sh to work with you on education issues."

I'm from a family of fourteen and one of the middle children of Hazel Pete and Joseph Dupuis. On my mother's side is Chehalis and Nisqually, and on my father's side, I am Potawatomi and Sac and Fox.

My older brothers were embraced by the Potawatomi people and carry names from the Prairie Band Potawatomi from Horton, Kansas. I traveled to meet my people there as an adult. Two in my family were adopted out. My brother was adopted by my mom's parents, and my sister was returned to us October 31, 1991. I have five sisters and two brothers still living. I was raised as the oldest daughter of a family of eight by my mom, a single parent.

That's who I am.

From Survival to Awakening

The Chehalis, like other tribes, were confronted early on with basic survival situations. Colonization and assimilation was the reality over a fifty-year period. In the early 1900s, White man diseases were decimating the few Chehalis remaining on the reservation. Boarding school for some of our children meant the difference between living and dying. Tuberculosis was the disease that forced Harriet and Frank Pete to send their children to boarding school.

Our tribe was resourceful, and it made a difference that we worked alongside White people in the few jobs that were available. But Chehalis men faced unemployment and underemployment. Still, our land is prairie land and our rivers are free-running and healthy so we could always feed our families. We had indigenous food and animals on the land, timber for firewood, and canoes to get to town.

The very hard times for many generations mean that today we weigh decisions about economic development in terms of how it will benefit the people. How will it allow the Chehalis to reclaim cultural arts, traditions, language, and protocols lost to the Chehalis? These days, our people say the cultural traditions have been sleeping and now we are waking them up!

This awareness of being competitive within White academics and then also being aware culturally within the tribal community... those two things are not very congruent. It's not like they come together and mean the same thing.

My Mother's Embrace

Both of my parents were boarding school survivors, and each had radically different experiences. Hazel Pete credits the boarding school for the opportunity to live. Tuberculosis was taking a great toll on the health and lives of the people. Had she stayed on the Chehalis reservation, she might have not survived. So, she and a brother were sent away to boarding school and a younger sister stayed home. She had a relatively good experience in boarding school. She made friends from all across the country as she attended boarding schools at Chemawa, then Tulalip.

Later, as a weaving family, we would be called onto reservations to work with people on basketry. One summer, when we were at Tulalip, we took a walk with one of the young women. We were on the bluff where the old Tulalip school is, looking down. We were soon to have one of the canoe journeys to Tulalip. The sky was full of seagulls. My mother said, "This brings back memories."

She said when she was a student there, Makah families in canoes came into that area to visit their children at the school. Travel on canoes goes according to the tide. They had arrived with the tide, but the tide was changing, and it was time to leave. The people from the school went down to gather the children, but the children didn't want to leave the beach. They didn't want to be left by their families. But the canoes had to leave, because the tide was going out. Eventually, the canoes got on their way.

"When you hear these seagulls," my mother told us, "That's what it sounded like when these little kids were crying down below."

She had walked down from the bluff, she explained. She was a class representative and a sergeant, one of the people that marched the groups around. That school used army style and protocol. She was one of the people that went down to the beach. She hugged a third grader. They became lifelong friends while they were at boarding school and remained in touch. So, we always had a place to stay when we traveled to the Makah reservation.

It makes me imagine that the boarding schools and the taking of our children was that fifth step of colonization. After they take the land, they take the resources, they take the legitimacy of thought, they take our traditional governance, and then they take the children. They were trying to separate tribal people from their Indian ways, but many individuals held on to their being. Whatever they had as Indians they left to their people, their grandparents, their aunts and uncles, and their parents; whatever they had, they kept and held it tight. So, I always think of that day with Mom and these young Makah kids who were coming up to that boarding school for the first time. That was representative of her life, which was to always embrace. She modeled that for us.

Larger Than Life

As young people, we watch our parents. My dad also represented himself in some of the ways he lived his life. He was gone a lot. He drank and could be abusive. I always thought to myself, I will never do that.

He was very tall, a six-foot-five Potawatomi. He was very good-looking, Mom always said. She was four-foot-ten, but she had said, "I'm going to marry a man who is tall, strong, and has perfect teeth," because those were the things she felt like she didn't have. When Joe Dupuis came to our reservation, here was this six-foot-five man working with our people. In that generation, not many were taller than five-foot-two. He would have a hoe and he would have to bend down to be out working the crops with everyone else.

Later, as I came to know my dad's upbringing and life, which he didn't talk about, I recognized the trauma that he survived while in boarding school. He and his sister and both of my parents lived into their eighties. My Aunt Gertrude, Joe Dupuis' full sister, lived to be in her nineties. A wealth of information came forward toward the end of his life and then after his life, so I had a better understanding.

Reflecting about my life in my forties or fifties, I considered that all of those things I always thought most about my dad were the things that I actually embodied, qualities that also made me strong.

For one, he could command an audience. He was a gifted orator. He could tell stories. He could help heal. He could give his opinions.

He could move a community to activism. He often was the camp organizer, like at the Pendleton Round-Up, a rodeo and powwow. He would arrive two weeks early and begin to put together the tepees and the dancers and all of the different people who have responsibilities there. He was that type of organizer, but it took him away from home so much. I didn't like that. Yet now I can be in front of a crowd and microphone and have no fear. I acknowledge that his ability, which I watched and embraced, became a part of my life.

> ***"The most important teachings are those you hear from your full-time caregiver, the one who raises you."***

Still, for the one central to my lifetime, I point to Hazel Pete, my mother. On the Chehalis Indian Reservation, we did not have a paved road, running water, or electricity. And we had eight children to raise. The most important teachings are those you hear from your full-time caregiver, the one who raises you. Hazel Pete was certainly that for us, mostly as a single parent.

Our Family's Routine

I grew up without electricity, running water, and there were no paved roads into the Chehalis Reservation. At the time, the 1950s to the '70s, the Chehalis had no money. We experienced poverty, social and economic deprivation, and the consequences of limited resources. To sponsor cultural family events on the rez, we held bingo night, craft sales, raffles, wrote small grants.

We were rich with salmon, deer, berries, camas, and water from a well that provided for the whole reservation. We were up at dawn to do chores, pack a lunch, and then on to our favorite spots on the reservation. We were expected to be home by dusk, before the fog set in, and get ready for the next day.

My dad was still living with us. My younger sister and I were up at four-thirty, helping him get the big potbelly fire going. You do that at sunrise. You get the fire going. You get water boiling. You get the food cooked. Then, still early, he would leave for whatever job he was doing. Usually it was logging camp, which is why we were up so early; we got the fire going before he left. My younger sister and I still have that routine. We call each other at five o'clock in the morning knowing that we're already up.

All my brothers are cooks. All my brothers know how to raise babies and young children, because when my mom left for the field as a migrant worker (she usually maintained three jobs), the brothers were the ones that helped raise us. When my daughters were starting to date and look for a future partner, that's what I would always say. Always look for an Indian man who is the oldest of at least five children because he'll be able to cook, clean, and raise kids.

Salmon River, Chehalis Reservation

Children of Hazel Pete

My mom was instrumental in us knowing all the families on the rez. We attended tribal general council meetings where the language was still spoken; at the time, there were ten fluent speakers. We knew the families who raced horses on the prairie, and we witnessed some of the last overland canoe races. We fished with our grandpa Frank Pete on the Black and Chehalis Rivers, selling our catch to Indian fish buyers. From a distance we watched the huge gatherings for *slahal* during our annual Chehalis Tribal Days.[1] We attended the little white church, the Shaker Church, and traveled to Skokomish for Seone, the traditional religion. We went to a school, and that was White culture. Outside the school day, we participated in a full spectrum of changing cultural times for the Chehalis tribe.

My mother was a certified instructor from the first graduating class of the Institute of American Indian Arts in Santa Fe. She left from boarding school, did her own application to the Institute, and was on a bus for three days to get down there. She graduated with her class. She then worked at Laguna Pueblo, then Riverside, California, and Warm Springs, Oregon. When the war started, people from our tribe were called to Seattle to work on munitions. Our people would pack the munitions and get them on the ships. My female cousins and sisters got a single apartment and worked in the

---

1 *Slahal* is a gambling game of the Indigenous peoples of the Pacific Northwest Coast, also known as stickgame, bonegame, bloodless war game, handgame, or a name specific to each language. In the Coast Salish tradition, the Creator gave stickgame to humanity as an alternative to war at the beginning of time. The game serves multiple roles in Native culture—it is at once entertainment, a family pastime, a sacred ritual, and a means of economic gain through gambling.

shipyards. That's what my mom did and that's how she met my dad, who was also working there.

My mom modeled an imprint of woman: resourceful, hardworking, with an ability to find humor in daily events and an ability to reframe situations, with optimistic willingness to help others, with faith and spirituality, with social support. She had the ability to face fear and the unknown. I think of these qualities as the ways of my people.

Modeling Chehalis Values

As an elder I model hard work, perseverance, and a steadfast commitment to reclaiming our cultural art traditions. I'm the middle daughter of fourteen. My youngest sister and I were early risers, always the ones to get things ready for the day. From spring into the early fall, that would mean getting ready for regular trips to gather basket supplies. We gathered cedar, cattail, sweetgrass, tulle, bear grass, and nettle.

Our people know how to persevere through all the times that teachers, agencies, and government officials have said no. We persevered through times when laws and policies were meant to hold the Chehalis tribe back. Myself, I persevered through the illogic of public schools to assimilate tribal people into White society.

Today, my daughters, grandchildren, and great grandchild live in rapidly changing times. My husband, Gary, and I voice concern and model for them that they have the obligation to provide for each other and for the needs of future generations. They have the significant responsibility to make plans, give voice to the vision, and provide the political, social, and spiritual groundwork for the seventh generation from now. They know this because we talk about it. They know that their actions and that their "stand" within their lifetime is important.

THE ONLY INDIANS

Our reservation is divided by a county line, with a few kids on the Grays Harbor side at that time. Most kids went to one district but my whole family, eight of us, were put in a different school district. We were the only Indians there. Because of this county line that divides the rez, my brothers, sisters, and I attended a school as the only Indians, with one Dupuis in each classroom.

My older brothers could have and should have told me what was going to happen on the first day of school, when you're in school surrounded by the children of Norwegian and Swedish immigrant parents.

We did not have kindergarten; we had first grade. The first day I got on the bus and went to Mrs. Ruggi. She had taught all of my older brothers. Most of my classmates were Swedish, so they're real platinum blond with white skin so thin that you can see their blood veins. They seemed so frail, I'm thinking, Oh, my God, their blood is going to just burst! Of course, I've been trained to be stoic, so I'm not exclaiming, not even with facial expressions.

We had Blue Boy pencils, probably as thick as your little finger. Mrs. Ruggi went around and touched each kid to show them how to hold it while they would write. When she got to me, she didn't touch me. It seemed like a signal to the other kids that there is something different about Yvonne Dupuis. It felt like she was going to be hands off with me, like she wouldn't be giving me an edge in anything.

In the case of our family, teachers failed to recognize that Hazel Pete's children knew how to read, write, and do some mathematics because she was a teacher. When we played at home, we played school because Hazel Pete was always about reading, writing, and knowing facts on the radio. Once we got a landline phone, she would always call in when the radio would have a contest and she'd know the answer.

It's that kind of modeling that prepares you. Even that first day of class, I proclaimed to myself in my head, so this is how it's going to be: Every gain that I make in this classroom will be because I'm forceful about it.

All of the reading and math groups were according to bird names. I could figure out which one was the top group. My goal was to be in these top groups. I would do that at six years of age. This sets in motion a momentum where it's about survival, gain, and being acclaimed somehow. From that first day of class, I had that awareness. I was driven. I was so competitive to be the top student that I lost the ability to be close friends with anyone.

The White kids seemed strange to me. I could not see that we had anything in common. It was only later, in high school, that several of my White acquaintances and I had a conversation. We had been in the same classes from first grade. One of the students talked about how she was amazed that I could talk about my parents being divorced and separated and my mom raising us. Another one offered that it was hard for her. Out of the seven young women sitting there, five were in homes where the father had left. I saw that, and thought, "Oh, my God, they have some of the life challenges that I have."

As a teacher working with young women, sometimes I will make a point to say, "I need the women to hear this and I'm only going to say it once: Hold tight to identity, but not so tight that you can't leave an opportunity to have a conversation with somebody else." To say, "Is this happening to you or this is happening only to me? So that you find the common thread that continues to be a basis for friendship."

Watch, Learn, Do

Hazel Pete taught us that we are just like all of the other families on the reservation.

As a colonized people, we had nothing. Then, when our grandparents were returning from boarding schools, they brought with them skill sets that would set into motion the planning to be ready for paved roads, running water, and electricity. The homes that those men built were ready for toilets and running water and bathtubs. The outlets were there for the electricity that they knew was coming (it just did not come for another twenty years).

But the idea was of group work, to better all the people on the reservation. There was never this idea of, oh, we're not going to go work on that house, they're not our relatives. Or, it's too far away. The opposite happened. They all came because they knew that they could either hammer, or they could read the plans, or they knew how to order the wood, or they would saw their own wood. Those were the skill sets that came home from the boarding school with our grandparents. Our own idea was of group work.

The other thing about our grandparents was they were observant, they spoke our language, and would be watchful for a career or experiences that they knew would be needed back on the reservation. Frank Pete, Hazel Pete's dad, my grandfather, was the first police officer. He became a federal officer and a judge on the reservation. He would travel to Tacoma and sit in the federal courthouse and watch the protocol. He worked at Cushman in maintenance so he would spend his days off going to the courthouse. That way he learned the protocol of how you give advance notice, how to keep a record, how to do this and that. When he became deputized and was serving on the Chehalis reservation, he became this respected individual that you would go to.

There would be other career-like activity that tribal people in my grandparents' and mom's generation invested in. They couldn't go to vocational school or college, but they could be watchful for how these jobs got accomplished. They imagined a role within the tribe, then watched for identifying the skill set they needed to learn, do, build, create, and network.

Salmon being smoked

Sitting Beside

I learned that cultural and formal education was important. I knew women were highly capable and could get an education, and a job, and then work to get others through college. Young people need to decide when to begin making a difference. But you can't simply leave; take time to learn through "sitting beside" to learn the arts, language, medicine, stories, songs, dances, and, very importantly, the protocols of our own people.

Oral tradition honors children as the vital link between the past and the future. Extended families recognize words and actions as forces that can be acted upon by the coming generations. Our ancestors lived in a tumultuous time. In the midst of that, they took the time to think about us, to try to provide the things we need to continue to live as Indians and to identify as Indians, including land;

political, social, and spiritual rights; rituals; symbols of culture; language; and memory of our rightful relationships to nature and to each other. Ours are the faces that our ancestors would never see, the names they would never pronounce, laughter they would never hear, tragedy they would never experience.

Weaving Honors Our Ancestors

Weaving, and the act of recognizing plants used in weaving, gathering, processing, designing, and actually weaving, is the cultural metaphor I use to inspire and actively cultivate resilience in my community. In the Puget Salish region, all Indians descend from a weaver, and I challenge first-time weavers to know who the weavers are in their family, then honor them by weaving.

Weaving is cultural knowledge, provides an income, links us to the past, and will link us to the future. It is a connection to our history, our language, and culture, and with each additional piece of knowledge our people become strong. Hazel Pete is quoted as saying, "We would weave with what was in our reach and today we reach around the world!" The spiritual father Skokomish said, "Artists were the first historians because artifacts can tell the history and culture of a people." When you begin to weave, all aspects of history and culture begin to fall in place. Ancestors applaud your waking up a cultural art form.

Weavers now are typically eighth, ninth, and tenth generation weaver families, since the negotiation of treaties in the Puget Salish area. This is important to know because our culture was nearly wiped out by laws, policies, and racism. The knowledge about history and culture gets passed down because basketry is a "sit beside" art, and "talk story" is the way elders, extended family members, and master teachers teach the importance of culture, history, and weaving as a political and cultural birthright.

> *"I've learned to be ready to accept a teaching,*
> *then work hard, persevere, and commit to reclaiming*
> *traditional arts of our people."*

When I became a certified teacher, I was totally committed to my classes. I didn't pay equal attention to weaving. Hazel Pete stopped me one day when I was leaving for another meeting and said, "Sit beside me because you need to learn this today!" It was an imbrication technique weaving bear grass into a sweetgrass and cattail basket. That is one afternoon the ancestors were applauding! Electricity passed from her to me as I took the basket and learned the weave. I've learned to be ready to accept a teaching, then work hard, persevere, and commit to reclaiming traditional arts of our people.

Mentoring Masters

Mentoring becomes full time in many ways because life happens and one becomes part of the life of an apprentice, with all its challenges, accomplishments, and work opportunities. The planning of ceremony, such as the acknowledgment of a Master Weaver, becomes all-encompassing. For instance, if the weaver does not carry an ancestral tribal name, that ceremony has to happen, too. They must make all the items for the giveaway, select witnesses from four directions, invite relatives to acknowledge the event, prepare the dinner, and adhere to the teachings of the spiritual father as he instructs them in the protocol of being brought out as a Master Weaver.

I mentored eight young weavers over three years to prepare them as Master Weavers. Several were part of my extended family and others were from neighboring tribes; we became family by the end of the three years because of the trips to the mountains, the ocean, prairies, mud flats, and rivers to gather. We shared food and talked story over the years as I mentored them in the art of basketry.

I'm now mentoring my thirteen-year-old grandson as he prepares to be brought out as a Master Weaver. He started to gather and weave when he was five and is now nearing the age for a tribal public acknowledgement of his work. Very few make the commitment to weave.

The Last Cedars

Our community is actually cedar poor as of three years ago. We had to harvest the last of our standing cedar trees. A White owner acquired it and was selling them for profit. They were to be felled. We were among several weavers that moved in to harvest that cedar. This big machine was coming to clear-cut everything; we literally were just three hours ahead of it.

The cedar stand was on the reservation, within walking distance of all of our homes, and then it was cut down. It hurt our connection to the earth when we saw the clear-cutting of the last grove of cedar trees on our traditional land.

We were in scramble mode to strip the felled trees and move the strips to where other people would take it and process it. When we did the final call, everybody came up on this ridge and we were looking down on this big machine that would take a tree, take off the limbs, take off the bark, and then it would be on the side. It would even start to stack them.

Our kids, even the six-, seven-, and eight-year-olds—it was the first time they saw a clear-cut on the Quinault reservation. One of the kids, and she was only seven, said, "I think I can hear them crying."

With us it's not just the act of protection, it's the act of sorrow when they take the last. That commitment to regenerate and plant is strong for our people because we know what being the last is. So now let's stop our sorrow. Let's now plant again so that those trees will be part of our family.

Tree Teachings

I had four tribal young people who were going to get cedar for the first time. We met early, at 6:00 a.m. We travel in a group and encourage others to travel in a group. Our meeting spot is usually at a McDonald's because we always get coffee, and that's the last time for the kids to use the bathroom. These days, even rez kids have a hard time going out in nature.

Our trip might be two or three hours up into the hills. We'll establish a camp, usually for the elders, but it could be young people as well. Any babies are left with us right at the camp. We'll have pop-up tents, tables, all of our tools, all of the lunch food.

We begin with a prayer to recognize the teachings of the tree people. In our area, the trees are seen as the first teachers. For every tree, there's a teaching that they give to us. When you look at the cedar, some of their upper limbs look like a person with elbows bent, hands raised, palms toward the body, which is the gesture that my tribal people use to express thanks. We raise our hands to thank the people and that's a teaching of the tree people. The tree says, I've raised my hands to thank you that you honor me and remember me as one of your teachers. Take my bark. Take my new growth. Take my limbs. Take my roots. They're for you. The Creator has placed me here because I am part of your support, part of your foundation.

That's what you pray for. We're also praying for the safety of our youngsters, teenagers, young twenties, even young thirties. They'll be working with knives to get that bark started. We have fashioned a crowbar so that it has an end that will start stripping on the tree. But then we also use the traditional tools, a root digger, to start the trees.

There are different ways for pulling the bark from the tree. For live trees, which are not going to be clear-cut, taken down, you can only take one-fourth or less. That's all you are to take so that the tree will live, the tree will survive. To guide people, we always say it's the measure of the palm.

One year, at Quinault, we were in the fullness of the gathering season. The sap would spray the people with a mist as they were pulling. That's a blessing from the tree to experience that, the love coming from the tree to you, as you pull the bark and wind it.

You take several strips, perhaps ten at a time. Can you imagine how heavy these are? And then you start to walk to the camp where we are, the people who are doing the next part of the process. Every puller is honored. We don't care if you're just bringing one piece or twenty, you are honored when you walk back into that camp.

The stripping and pulling of the bark—for the first ones who go out, it's a time they will never forget. We have elders who went maybe once as a small child, but they can still tell you how to do it. That's the survival of the information. Even through public school and boarding schools—let's say you're removed from those teachings for ten years—but you did it before you left, you know one piece. That's why our people need to return. They have a part of the teaching. They might have a phrase for what it was called. They might even have the song or the origin story. That's how we have all of these pieces of the puzzle now. It is this generation's work to bring it all together, to make it whole.

Reclaiming Connectedness

We were with Quinault people on this place called "the wedge" for its shape. Although people still call it the wedge, that place is clear-cut now. That time, we were so excited to be there that everybody got out of their cars, grabbed the tools, and walked out. We didn't take the water or the food because we felt we could get back and forth. But apparently we're not a generation that easily can determine north, south, east, and west. No one knew later where the cars were parked! We just walked and walked.

In there, all of us were together. We had a separate camp set up within the circle of the trees that people were gathering. I was not an elder then, but the cedar bark was heavy. The cedar is wet; it has all the sap in it. Even younger kids were carrying more than one hundred pounds.

It's draped on your back, draped on the front, and others are helping tie it on you. It's even under your arms. As we began to move, I thought we probably looked like elephants with their big strides. We would get to a log that was down and we would have to figure out how to get over. We were relying on one of the young men to climb a tree, to be guessing the right direction to get to our cars. It's a full emotive feeling of doing the work of our ancestors. You just knew the ancestors are having a big laugh about us, like, hey, they don't even know where their cars are. They don't know where north is!

So, we learn. Doing the activity is what sets that emotion of cultural fullness, that you're complete. It's not just survival, but that the knowledge is still intact. We have the cedar one more time. Because there were generations of weavers that did not have cedar, did not have sweetgrass, did not have cattail because of how colonization takes away the legitimacy of our thought. If the Chehalis thought they were weavers, then the boarding school's mission was to eradicate that. If the Chehalis people knew about the connectedness to plants and trees, the colonizer tried to sever all of that connection back to the traditional cultural knowledge. That's the reclaiming aspect of today's generation. It becomes their work to listen, watch, and then put all of those pieces together to make it whole again.

Bringing Cedar Home

Those times, we would return home with a pickup load of cedar. Hazel Pete would still be up at midnight, waiting for us. She literally would start doing the final separating of the outer bark and the inner bark. It's the inner bark that you want to use that gets rolled up. That's what's hung in the carport area, so that it's wind dried. The bark would be mounded like a huge molehill. To see her start on that huge pile, we would think she just wanted to get her hands on it and then go to bed. Oh, no. She'd have the lights on and be working throughout the night. Then, the next day, we could see where we were supposed to start in.

These days, we have a particular drop place for all of the cedar that's coming in and being brought back. Although sometimes, in gathering, we are able to keep up with the pullers and get it stripped even before we leave a location. That's the goal. But if we don't, when we bring it home, it's ready to be soaked, so the person who's doing the final stripping can complete it within three days. You're always keeping track of when the cedar was gathered. We mark everything and log it in location. We keep track of who was on the gathering trip, because if they aren't weavers, they will get a basket. They get something in return for helping us out, although they're just grateful for the experience and the knowledge to have been there.

A Gift of Camas

Over time, remembering has become an intimate process for my family. "I remember…" and "remember when…" are phrases that trigger talk story. The things that are remembered most often are funny, generally purposeful for their instructive purpose, or tragic in that a comparable incident will not be repeated again and so must be remembered.

Each spring the camas blooms. Usually, it appears in May. It is an exciting time because it signifies the start of the season for gifts from the East, the sun. Renewal, innocence, guilelessness, spontaneity, joy, and the capacity to believe in the unseen are connected feelings and beliefs of what the gathering of camas represents for the Chehalis. My sister asked if we remembered when the kids went to pick camas. We do. She gives voice to the story. "I was busy," she recalled, "We were all busy, but the kids wanted to pick camas but no one was able to take them. They returned later in the afternoon, however, after having walked to the prairie, taking the root bags and digger, and brought back a gift of camas for everyone."

They were ages three and six. The reason for picking camas is already part of their soul. It says, I'm willing to share knowledge, wisdom, and the lived experience of myself, family, and people.

Making a Master Weaver

In a public ceremony, when my daughter was in eighth grade, she was brought out by the Skokomish smokehouse people and the tribe as a Master Weaver.

There were several criteria that my daughter had met, including gathering, pounding, and then weaving a cedar garment. The smokehouse father, who was also a weaver, helped put the finishing touches on that day as she was brought in a circle to the four directions, to be proclaimed as a Master Weaver. This was also a recognition of her entering adulthood, where there would be things that she would now be expected to accomplish and pay attention to. We're moving her from childhood then into young womanhood.

In trying to capture for others what they could establish as criteria, we always looked at it in terms of seven. It's the seven teachers that have been instrumental in coming to know how to identify the weaving plants, how to keep them healthy, how to be the protector of these plants and trees and bark and roots, and then how to gather, process, and prepare.

These skills that you have been taught, what will you be masterful about? You get to choose one. That's one of the teachings of our people. They say that you don't teach everybody the same thing because then they won't need each other. So even though we have many people who are masterful, and master teachers using cedar bark, many of them have a different technique that they have become masterful about. I have a sister who is very accomplished with multiple techniques and she always writes things down in her recipe book: the plant, the beans, the season, and who taught her.

> ***"Our people say that you don't teach everybody the same thing because then they won't need each other."***

Another criterion is that as the person moves forward in their own work, they're always acknowledging their first teacher, the ancestral teaching. It goes way back to a point in time where we're not even knowledgeable about where this information came from.

My grandson's specialty is a weave we always thought only occurred in northern tribes, say Swinomish and Tulalip North. Now the archaeological digs that have occurred right here in our Puget Sound-Salish Sea area tell us that the technique was also rich here some ten thousand years old. That's why it came relatively easy to him and he specialized with it, as did Hazel Pete.

You acknowledge your teachers because that recognizes the ancestral knowledge all the way back to the beginning. It would have involved insects, birds, sometimes even the four-legged who have offered us their antlers for tools, their bones for needles and awls.

We're thankful to all of the life force around us when someone becomes a Master Weaver. We value that the person carries their tribal name. By the time they come out as a weaver, they've gone through that ceremony. The reason that tribes will establish their own sense of who their Master Weavers are is because it's in our recorded history.

Coming out as a Master Weaver has a reward that's connected to identity. Knowing that, this is a gift. Because now you carry this label of Master Weaver, one of your obligations is to make sure more weavers are coming up and coming into their own in terms of knowing the plant and animal life that contributes to what you need as a weaver.

Mother Earth, Protected and Kept Viable for the Generations

Some time ago, elders were interviewed about concerns on climate change. The tribe inquired about climate change and the future for the Chehalis tribe. A group of young people put together a questionnaire and wanted our questions.

As a Master Weaver, one of the questions that I posed was: Is there an awareness of the significant change there has been to our basketmaking material? Other questions that I thought would be valuable: During your lifetime, what have been the protocols that you know our people practiced so that the plants would return from one season to the next? What is it that we do? What are the laws and policies? What is your lived experience with these actual written-down laws that are either within the tribe or within local, state, or federal laws that protect plants, because for us, it's a treaty right. The treaty right in this area is from the Stevens Treaties; the picking of berries and plants is guaranteed within our treaty.[2]

We have fought for our fishing rights as far as the United States Supreme Court. I see us moving forward within my lifetime to protect

---

2 The Stevens Treaties are several treaties negotiated with Native nations in what was then Washington Territory. They were signed by Governor Isaac Stevens for the United States, and included the Treaty of Hellgate (1855), Treaty of Medicine Creek (1854), and Treaty of Neah Bay signed with the Makah (1855).

our plants, the way we eat them, use them for medicine and ceremonies, industry, and weaving.

We hear about forest fires in the media. Among people who gather, we know all of those trees that have provided medicine. The whole plant is sacred, and I mean the bark and the root or the different ways that we use it within ceremony. Our stories tell us about the plant life that are protectors for the other medicines that grow within this forest environment. It's not just trees that are in the forest. There are these smaller plants that tribal people have used as the medicine to keep us well not just physically, but also emotionally—that mind-state presence that you need for prayer. This is for the prayer that is so powerful that it can provide the way for us to see into the future. The gatherers were the first to say that we lost all that nettle or devil's club.

There's a reason for us to work in full circle with the environment. Humans are not at the top of the food chain. We're probably way at the bottom. All of that needs to come full circle, that recognition of how we're part of the circle and that's all we are. Our part is seeing the way to keep this plant, that this world is protected and viable for the future, not just for my children and grandchildren and great-grandchildren—since I now have a great-granddaughter—but the generations I will not see.

Tribal people recognize that we need to carry the names forward. I think about when we have lost a name and we need to state the name. Because their work was that important, say the name into the future so that it lasts for seven generations. If I have done my work well enough, my name will carry into the seventh generation.

"Building bridges is most important—always preparing our young ones to meet the world."

BARBARA POLEY

Laguna/Hopi

B ARBARA POLEY has faithfully seeded the Hopi way of life for decades with community-minded dedication. She gathered strength from Hopi values and skills that her parents instilled in her to overcome marginalization, earn a bachelor's and master's degree from Northern Arizona University, and live a life of service.

Barbara's two decades of leadership at the Hopi Foundation brought forward the educational ethics of her ancestor, the revered chief Loloma. Among many contributions, she developed a leadership curriculum that has empowered dozens of Hopi thinkers, doers, and dreamers to heal and guide others. She instituted a truly dynamic and respectful way to work with people in their own communities. The next generation of leaders is rising throughout Hopi, growing strong with Barbara's guidance toward self-determination.

Barbara moves into the next phase of her elderhood, putting energy toward expanding the fundamental idea of caring for one another across generations. "When we have self-identity and have our values as our shield," she reminds us, "We create resilience for our Hopi way of life, taking into context the many present changes in society that we have been dealt. The renewed strength of our people will lead toward our survival for generations to come."

Doubly Good

I come from two tribal memberships. My mother is Laguna from New Mexico, and my father is Hopi from the Hopi reservation. Having been born into two tribal memberships, as many of us are, we are taught from both sides beginning in our early years. I was brought up to know how the Laguna is supposed to act in public or with the family, and how the Hopi handles similar situations. As I was taught, I feel like I was double exposed to learning how to be a good person. I feel good about that.

I had my Laguna grandparents, who lived about two miles from where my family lived in the small town of Winslow, Arizona. My father was Hopi, yet his training background was high school up to the tenth grade, in California. My mother's background was finishing up to the eighth grade in a Catholic school in the town of Ganado on the Navajo reservation.

Hopi village

OUR VALUES

In a family with two cultural backgrounds and two different Native languages, and with the pressures of life, my parents did not have the opportunity to spend time fully learning each other's languages. They spoke English in the home. During that time, my parents felt it was important to train their children to speak English to be able to do well in education, and succeed in the school system. This was their priority and that was their choice. So we as children were not taught either language. I do know some basic Hopi and Laguna—the greeting words. But I used to feel in my younger years that I was left out because I didn't learn as deeply in either language.

What I did learn, and it is just as good as learning the language, is what the values mean from both sides, from both of my peoples. They're pretty similar. Learning and teaching others about our values has become really important in my life.

Over time, in thinking about how to share our culture with our own people, I became aware that I was teaching our traditional values. I had not realized how much I was already teaching values in my work time. It was just in the way I handled the staff and the relatives that I met. Those were all values that my parents and grandparents taught me.

> *"Learning and teaching others about our values has become really important in my life."*

A Rich Family

My Hopi grandparents could not speak English. We would come to the Hopi reservation to visit from my birthplace in Winslow to the Hopi reservation about one hundred miles away. We would visit maybe every three months or so if we could. In those early years it was all dirt roads coming out to the reservation. I remember the travel because you got to sit in the back in the small truck and be nice and dusty when you got to my Hopi grandparents' home. It was the best time.

My grandmother had a back problem that was never corrected, so she was bent over. She used a little stool to get herself around the house. She never went to the hospital. My grandmother would make the best biscuits and she knew about what time we'd show up, so you could smell it coming in the door. She'd have that ready for us, with a big smile, and her greeting in Hopi. Even though we spoke different languages, I learned how to communicate with my grandparents in a way that I felt loved. And I hope I showed them love.

My grandfather could talk a little bit of English, and he'd just say, "We need to prepare to go out to the orchard," which was a little distance from their home. We would have to pick the fruit. He would just be so happy to have a little bit of help to bring in the harvest. We did those kinds of things as children. I am first remembering the happy times, the really, really happy times, even when not being able to speak the language.

My other grandparents lived near us, in Winslow. They had been sent out of their area to work on the railroad. They were called "boxcar" Lagunas. The Santa Fe railroad made a deal with the tribe to provide employment to Laguna people. Many Laguna people in Winslow and a few other places around Arizona and California came out for those jobs. It was at an area where they had a lot of traffic for trains. Boxcars were put up as housing. That's where my grandfather worked. I never saw the boxcars as boxcars. I had no idea that's what they were until someone wrote about them. All I had known is that we had enough room for a kitchen, bathroom, two bedrooms. My grandparents, because my grandfather was a little higher on the Santa Fe line, got to have at least four boxcars that made a house for the family. The rest of the people who lived down the rows only had two boxcars. So I came from a rich Laguna family.

A Home on Hopi

In my early years, the 1950s, with roads not being paved, you spent a lot of time on the road—a lot more time than we do now. From Hopi, we now spend an hour going to Winslow, an hour and a half going to Flagstaff. Hopi land is located in the northeast part of Arizona. If you look at a map and find the location, we're inside a circle that surrounds us—that is Navajo land. There's a long story to that.[1]

Hopi differ from Navajo in the way we live. Hopi lived together, really close together, in villages. Navajo, because of their style of having sheep in the early years, had to roam here and there to find

---
1 Navajo-Hopi land

pastures for their animals. Navajo lived in a lot of different locations surrounding us. I can't remember the miles of Hopi land but we still remain close together because we do live on three mesas: First, Second, and Third Mesa. I live on Third Mesa and the village I come from is named Bacavi. That is the village of my husband's family. Culturally, when you live on Hopi, you are supposed to be moving to your wife's location. My family home is still in the Third Mesa area but it is the lower part called Kykotsmovi, where most of my blood relatives live.

When my husband, Orin, and I finally started thinking about really having a home somewhere I had to always remind him that I wanted to live on higher ground, on a mesa. Because he cares and loves me so much, he went to his relatives to see about this request. It's a request that he probably didn't want to make because he knows the cultural way. But I'm also from a different tribe. He could tell them, She's from Laguna, so she wants this.

Luckily his aunts talked about it at the time and told him about an orchard where his grandfather used to do a lot of planting and it is outside of the village. They said, "If that's a place you want to fix up, then we'll give that to you." He looked it over, and we started moving up here. We've been in our new location more than ten years now. When we moved here not only did he do an addition to the trailer we brought here but he also started looking at the plants that might still be able to live. He's a great farmer. He was able to bring back to life at least four cherry trees. People didn't know we had cherry trees up here. We have a huge grapevine outside. I'm always calling people now, to come and help themselves. He revived a lot of the trees—peaches, apricots—surrounding our place. I know his grandfather would be thankful for what he has done because that's part of the life of Hopi.

CORN: A LIFEWAY ALL ITS OWN

Dryland farming has a lot to do with the religion of the Hopi people. I think that has created the emphasis on having our ceremonies. Praying for rain was already there, but receiving help from the clouds and the Creator above was even more important. The rainfall in our area is only about eight inches per year. The farmers had to find the valleys between the mesas. They learned where the water flowed when we did have rain, and that's where they set up their fields.

My husband's field is about six miles from our home. He would go there daily, sometimes twice a day, morning and evening, when he's planting, and when he's waiting for the plants to come up. The people provide prayers and have ceremonies for the rains. We begin praying for moisture through our kiva ceremonies that start in December. Then we have *kachina* dances, the outside plaza ceremonies. Through these spiritual beings, with the prayers and the songs for creating the rain, we seek the moisture that we need; that's all in those ancient songs that are being sung.

There is a part where sometimes I can feel left out. When you don't know the language, you don't understand the words to those prayers. I was able to ask my husband to explain to me the words of those songs that are sung. That's how I learned the importance of the songs. I could pay more attention as we were sitting out there in ceremony. You have to be in a good space to help our spiritual beings, to pray for the necessity of moisture for our country.

And we still live here. We still get corn, which is the main item that we grow. Over hundreds of years we still have the corn coming in and we continue drying the corn so it can be used for years to come.

Right now, we have had less and less rain. Some people in different parts of the reservation have a good crop, which is great. So I know what person I'm going to call on if I need some. I'll put an emphasis on them. But they do that for me, too, and during the years when they don't have any blue corn, or white corn, I offer them my corn.

Sometimes people will call and ask if they can buy some corn. For us, we don't sell the corn. That's the White man's way, to pay for something. Those of us who are older like to barter. If a person that I know has some skill that I might need, I might ask them for help later on, but I would never take money for anything that I gave, especially corn or beans.

That ancestral thinking is beginning to change. I watch that when I look at Facebook and I see the young people asking for things like "I want to buy some corn." It's not that simple. People have to begin to recognize how many months it takes to do the planting, to care for the plants, to do the harvesting. And when you're done harvesting, how to put that corn away so that it lasts for years and years to come.

Those are values that I think we are beginning to lose because we're not including the young people enough in the process of the life that sustains us.

Elder Wisdom

I try to advise our young people to make sure they spend some time with their elders, their aunts and uncles. Ask them some questions, not too many at once. As we grew up we were taught not to question, but to listen.

"Elders have a lot of good words to say."

I learned in the workplace as I encountered people who were going for higher education that once they got through their higher education, they were highly anxious to do well, and that's a good thing. But some of them have forgotten how to reconnect to elders, and how to listen well. Elders have a lot of good words to say.

Listen well, and internalize. I think most of our people will recognize that what was done for and by Hopi, the survival of Hopi, the laws they developed for themselves, were based on simple things to keep people alive, keep people in good order. It's a system that was created as most community systems are created. The highest value is to take care of one another.

The whole basic way of living is in the minds of the elders. They won't say it in those same words, but they will tell you a story and those are the best things to listen to. Ask them: In earlier days, what did you do or use when you were making a cake? Where did you have to get your product? It will help the young ones come back from thinking, I just go to the store nearby; I pick up this canned product; I pick up these vegetables that are there. They need to wonder, How do these things grow? How did these foods get into the can? When they start questioning the end product, they start learning about the process that takes place.

Piki bread

I've known many grandparents in our community who take care of their grandchildren. Some of them are really good at it; they are good at expressing how they feel about them. If the child wants to do something or learn something, they're there to make it happen. I've seen a few of those grandparents and their grandchildren—they are really strong together. The grandchild will grow up and never forget what the grandmother did for them. We have children who lose some of this connection with their own parents because their parents are working, or they're gone. The grandparents take over some of the education and connection that's needed by grandchildren. Grandparents sometimes feel like, "Oh, I might just spoil my kids," not realizing what they're doing is actually giving as much love to them as they can, so that child can grow up remembering that somebody cared for them.

My Strongest Influence

"That's another early lesson: you need your people; you can't do things alone."

I got a lot of my early training from my father. My father, Abbott Sakiestewa, was very, very special. He treated all our relatives wonderfully. I observed him when people came to visit and could see how he treated them and how they responded to him. That was important to my early growth and development.

I was inspired that my father started our family business and worked with people who came into the curio shop. I was inspired to want to reach out and work with people. Just watching him with people led me to consider how I might do something in the future: What do I need to prepare myself in order to make sure I can get people to work with me, in a humanly, timely way? Because—and that's another early lesson—you need your people; you can't do things alone.

My mother, Ruth Day Sakiestewa, was quiet and she did a lot of the home duties that needed to be done. She was always busy doing that. My mother was a person who could teach me how to become skilled in cooking and sewing. To this day, those aren't my favorite things to do. But my father was very interested in making sure I became educated at a higher level than him, higher grades than him, so that my chore or desire was to continue teaching others. Don't keep it to yourself. Always make sure you train other people, or teach other people, to know how to make themselves better. That's what I learned from him. I had his encouragement to be in school, stay in school, do all my work, and get the grades I did.

I was looking through old photographs recently. I found my high school diploma, and my master's diploma as well. I have my father to thank for that. After he left us at such a young age, if I didn't think of those early words of his, I would not have been able to get through all of my higher education.

Once I started practicing what I observed my father doing, the way he treated people, I saw I could work with people. It built my confidence. I was learning by beginning to think, What more do I need to know about the people that I come from? Who am I? What makes me have the knowledge that's important that other people should know about us? So they can respect the way we live, the culture we have.

Innate Confidence

I was among just a very few young Native people who joined organizations at my school. I worked to move up into what they deem as higher levels of education. I worked to get into an honor society.

Those names or titles never meant anything to me. I don't like titles. I don't remember people's titles. I'd rather know their name and their face, and usually first names. What meant more to me was that by speaking with clarity, the older administrators with the title, say, of president or vice president, would call on me to ask for my opinion. I realized this was because they didn't know anything about our people. I worked to become good in school with so many people who had no idea who we were. I was on the move on my own to learn and know abilities that I could utilize within an organization.

In my young thirties, I was chosen as executive director at Native Americans for Community Action in Flagstaff. That was my first administrative job. It came with about twenty-eight staff people, and I was responsible for a budget of 2.5 million dollars. I took that job at NACA because I was motivated by the work and services of that organization. Our mission was to help our people cultivate themselves into doing better with their life skills and improving their employment.

I had only been there for one year, in a lower position, when the executive director position became vacant. The people searching for candidates on behalf of the board told me they thought I was ready for it. I wasn't sure if I was. I just said, "I can do it."

I didn't have administrative training. I just threw myself into it. It was a learning-on-the-job experience. But I could do it because I based myself firmly in the skilled training I received throughout my younger life of how to work with people, especially how to listen, because that's where you find out, first, what is in their background. Where is this individual coming from?

I felt confident because there was already a team. I would have enough people around me who are skilled in various things, and with those people, I thought, I'm going to be okay. I already knew I didn't have all the skills that were needed. But I did have the skill to work well with people. If you find a team and you work with that team, you learn about what they do best.

Seeking Healing

I wish I had stayed longer at that position, but throughout life, the needs of family can overwhelm as conditions change. By that time, my parents had succumbed to alcohol. My mother was still living with me and needed much daily attention. I had this new job, and I had to tend to her, looking for her after I got off of work, finding her, getting her home and just taking care of her. It became a really high-stress time.

At that same time, I also took in two of my younger nieces. They were both under ten years old. Their father was abusive to them and I would not stand for that. So I had those additional stresses that came onto me.

Until then, I didn't know what stress was. It put me in a downturn while I was still in that position of executive director. Luckily in that organization we had a counseling program. I was able to go in and tell its director I needed some help. When you get into a strong depression stage, you cry at any little thing. That's what happened to me. That's why I can recognize when people get into those stages. But my own guidance director was the one who helped me find somebody, outside the organization, to help me get some healing.

Empathy Is Necessary

As I moved through life, when I started looking for people to fill in different positions of our organization, there were very important questions for me to ask. Usually people would come in and say, "Well, these are my skills at the work I've been doing." And I would tell them, "I can see your skills on your resume. I'd also like to know what you do in your family. How do you take care of your family? What do you do in your village? How do you help? What have you done voluntarily?"

That tells me more about a person than their resume might. It takes all types of skills in life to work well for the people. Empathy is needed. That one takes a little bit longer to develop, because you have to begin to understand what empathy means for you and from you. We have to know how to listen, how to empathize.

I learned to sense that over a period of time. When staff would come to me with personal situations, I'd spent a little more time with them, doing heavy listening, making sure they said what they needed to say. I would ask a few questions to help them know and feel that I was concerned and that I was really interested.

Many times I found people would cut others off if they come in with those kinds of personal stories. I feel that is not the thing to do, not when you're trying to build people, when you're trying to create a cohesive group to do the work that needs to be done.

"It takes all types of skills in life to work well for the people."

Listening has been a high priority in my lifetime. People would look at me sometimes at the end of meetings, and ask me, "How come you never say anything when we're having these meetings?" I would just tell them, "Because it's important to hear from everyone." In doing that, there's less chance for people to start squabbling within your meeting time. If you don't listen and you cut them off quickly, that individual holds onto those feelings. As the director of an organization, it's important to have your ears open to everyone.

The Hopi Foundation

In 1985, there was a community foundation to build at Hopi. A small staff got the Hopi Foundation going: myself, the bookkeeper, and then associate director, Loris Taylor.[2] Both Loris and I had just completed working for tribal government, after four years. We accepted the new positions in late December 1990.

There were just the three staff and a board, and we were only supposed to work part time, to be part-time directors-in-training of the organization. That's why we took on that work. We said, "We'll do it together only part time, and then you'll have time to find a full-time director." My brain at that time was still trying to come down from working four years with tribal government. I knew I did not want to work for tribal government. Even though there wasn't as much money coming into a nonprofit foundation, the opportunities that lend themselves to creating possibilities for the community are more open.

The Hopi Foundation was small but we raised funds in a way that kept independence. We sought and accepted only funds that supported our program as we designed it, as we listened to people. That

---

2 The Hopi Foundation, founded in 1985, serves a population of 7,000 Hopi people in twelve villages.

was important to us. You have to know what you're dealing with from your community. You have to understand those real needs.

People with funds who wanted to tell us what and how to do it, and said this is some money we have for you to do it this way, we immediately shut them off. We would not go further with them. No, they had to take us seriously about how much we knew about what our community needed. Loris and I would say, "When you're ready to give money to this certain thing that we're talking about, then please come back and see us." That approach worked better than most people think.

Our community could tell us what they needed. You don't shove it down their neck. I found that was very important. Don't shove things down people's throats if they are not interested.

A Respectful Approach

We have twelve villages in Hopi. As we got established, if people could not find what they needed from the tribe, they would come to our organization. I'd sit with them and the first thing I'd ask is, "What are you bringing to the table?" I wanted to know their skills that might apply to what they requested for the village. Those are questions that they don't normally get. If you allow them to speak first, then you as the representative of the organization can tell them what kinds of things we offer.

Our approach was that we can help you find the funds that might be needed but we don't go into the village and give directions. That's the training we did with all developing leadership. Instead, we asked them to work *with* us. If we got the funds in, their project was their responsibility. We weren't going to go and get involved in each of those twelve villages. That was important.

If you don't train people in leadership positions to work within their own village, then you are stuck as an organization they become dependent on, constantly trying to be that one they look to for information and guidance. Our best contribution was training the village leadership, a couple at a time, in how they might present to their community. So we would give them some ideas, maybe some language, with a little training to improve capacity. We'd say, "This is for you to become the knowledge person to work within your community. More things can get done. You can have us there, at village meetings, we will listen, and we can work with you after the meeting, and we'll talk to you about other projects you need to do." They would be the ones to make those ideas come true with the rest of their village people. They liked that. It's a respectful approach.

All kinds of issues and ideas came from inside the communities. Some were small—maybe some help to fix up a building. These were small things until they felt the confidence that they could do more. As others began to listen to them and engage with them, they started coming back with bigger ideas, like helping to renovate and revise clan houses. Those are very important and they are found in each of these communities. And so community leaders had to find workers, and they had to understand how that clan house was built from top to bottom. We could get the special outside consultants who could tell us how specific aspects needed to be done, but they didn't have that connection to the meaning of clan houses that the community people had.

We worked like a connector for outside people and the community. The outsiders taught our workers many things, but they also learned about what it takes to build within a community, how it has to stop for ceremonies, that it has to have their prayers and cultural requirements. They learned much about our culture.

One of the state granting organizations did not want to learn about our culture. They wanted things done by a certain time of year. We ended up meeting with the agency people and we expressed to them, this is how it works here, and this is what you have to understand. They didn't want to extend the time to allow us to use the funds, but we got the extension.

The other thing they wanted was some kind of sign in that clan house that says, "Renovated with funds from" so-and-so. They wanted to be recognized. We told them in a nice way: that's not our way. They understood. We offered, "We can recognize you in our reports when we talk to people, but we're not going to put those kinds of signs that you do in other places in the city. That's just not going to happen." In time, they understood, and they stayed with us.

We had to educate people in some funding sources. One example was when we went to the state department in Phoenix and offered our formal presentation to give them a little bit of background on what it means to live on Hopi and some basics on culture. We said as we came home, "If they don't understand our way of life and don't want to work with us now, we'll find some other way." Some people will use their way of doing things in the city as leverage when they think they have the upper hand, because they have the money. But with us at the Hopi Foundation, that was not the case. Those kinds of detours didn't prevent us from moving forward. They just made us stronger at negotiating our terms.

I spent eighteen years with the Hopi Foundation. I had the experience of building up an organization. I wasn't the founder. I was a builder of the organization, with Loris, who had the policy field behind her. For that I was doubly happy, to have her connection with this organization. I didn't enjoy policy development. I still don't! I can talk about different ways that people do things and like for others to be able to say, well, this policy would help you immensely. I might say, "Do it, write it!" Then, I'll see if it feels right to me.

That is how I worked with policy development people and with legal people—if they didn't listen to me and they're coming back, trying to throw something different back on me, I don't need to listen to them anymore. That's just how I worked my way forward, learning how to find people who had the strong skills I didn't possess.

A Bridge for the People

We worked to help our own people. Our people tend to be always talking, upset with the tribal government. They don't like to go to the government. Loris and I came from working with the tribal government. We would not hesitate to ask people, "Did you know about this program they have under the tribal government?

And did you see them or talk to them?" We would say, "Okay, if you haven't gone to the tribal program departments, we know that they do this type of work." We'd sit down as a team and help the requester create that relationship with a program. We gave encouragement by saying, "What you're telling me is important, and we don't have the funds to help with a large project." We were part of helping them become connected to the tribal programs that were already doing some of the work that was needed.

2006-2007
Hopi Leadership Program
Field Trip

We didn't try to anger anyone or criticize the government because we had just come from working for tribal government. Having worked in the chairman's office for four years, we knew there were good programs and good people in most of the programs. It's just that our tribal governments sometimes don't know how to communicate appropriately.

We were a small nonprofit organization and we didn't have the kind of funds that the tribal government receives. We never received tribal government funding for any of the work that we did.

Tribal government just didn't see nonprofits as being strong enough for them to connect. They are seeing it now, with the pandemic. But before, when I was employed by a nonprofit in my early years, in my opinion, they didn't see it.

Demanding Respect at Work

I think working in tribal government strengthened us as women. It helped us become stronger for our community because we had to deal primarily with the men who worked throughout almost all of the tribal government and in the programs.

When Loris and I were staff assistants for the chairman, we would go out and meet with department people. During a department meeting, one of the more vocal men was sitting next to Loris. She was going to get her coffee and he said, "Oh, while you're up there you can get mine, too." And again, it's just the way he put it. Not "Would you get me some?" but "You can get mine, too." That ticked her off, but she was very calm. She calmly said back to him, "Oh, well, if you need some, then it would be nice for you to get my coffee, too. So we'll both have coffee together. Thank you very much."

I could never forget her being able to say that to him. I learned a lot of things from her about how to say no, how to be stronger just by watching her. She's a very strong, intelligent person, among other strengths. That's how we had to work with the staff of our tribal government in our early years. We never were approached in that manner again because everybody laughed at him, not her.

Lived Lessons

Here's another thing to think about: tone of voice when communicating. How are you saying things to somebody? How does it come out from you? We don't teach our people nearly enough to practice that. We'd benefit by having little sessions where you can practice that with each other. I was learning by experience and this is what I put into the leadership program that we all worked to create.

Those are early experiences that teach you, if you listen and watch people when they're working with somebody else. You start thinking (at least I did) that if they had only said it *this way*, they would have gotten what they needed. But then you start seeing why people don't express themselves, especially at meetings with tribal council. At that time, almost all the tribal council members tended to come down harsh on different issues. That's just their background experience and training. But it's like they feel they're an authority in something so they use a harsh way to show what that authority means. But it comes out wrong. I know that if we can learn how to communicate appropriately with one another, we would get more things accepted and done. That's still a hard one to watch, how we just have not learned how to communicate in a better manner.

When we were doing projects or we were talking to our community, we had both men and women coming to us who had projects that they were working on. We worked toward making people feel we worked as a team, that both genders had capacity and intelligence. Our working style provided our male consultants and those on our staff to recognize the intelligence we had as female leaders in the workplace.

These are all lessons. When you work with people in your own best ways of thinking or being, and when you train people in that manner, they watch you, they observe you, they listen to you. Those become trainings for other people who need to hone their own skills to be able to do better work in the community.

I didn't realize that until later on, but I see that's what I had been doing with many of my staff, because they worked well with the community. That was the lived lesson I tried to impart. I opt to try to give our people a way to build up their confidence if I observed their intelligence was high in the various projects that we assisted them to complete by allowing them to take the lead. That's why I like to learn about people, because I have to know where they're coming from. If I know their strengths, then I can help build up their confidence better.

Contribute to Your Community

Building bridges is most important—always preparing our young ones to meet the world. I am happy to have higher education. I really feel good about our young people having that desire, too. But I always tell them: Don't think institutional learning is the only way to be present in life. Living in a community will provide each one of us with experiences to understand the values and desires of their location, to listen intently and ask questions. That community also needs to learn about you, your childhood, your parents, the structures in your life. One's value doesn't start with getting those higher education degrees but with how your life was shaped after you graciously came into this world. We should be more attentive as we listen to learn, so we don't miss the things that should be most important to us.

Afterword

SPIRIT ALIGNED – A PASSION FOR SHARING

In 2015, I had the privilege to walk into a room filled with some of the most powerful souls in the universe. They all sat in a circle and greeted me like elders sometimes do—with a smile. I was there to film them, to document this meeting of women leaders from all over the world. It was a sobering experience to be there within that energy, to see their eyes watching me, to hear their voices coming from home. It was an early indication of what I would be doing for the next eight years, making sure that we could see their presence and hear their voices.

It is thus gratifying for me to now write the afterword to their book, *Worlds within Us*, edited by Katsi Cook, and encompassing the eight life narratives of these terrific Native women elders.

In the next years, I spent many weeks with the first standard bearers of the Spirit Aligned program. The eight women chosen were selected because of their many years of work within their own communities, and the individual power and strength that each one holds. I knew that my work would go far beyond just following everyone around with a camera. I was there to tell their stories and to ensure that the world had a glimpse into the work that they do, but more importantly to document the lessons held within those images for use in their own communities.

I immediately gravitated toward Dr. Henrietta Mann because she reminded me so much of my own grandmother, her gentleness and electricity so well blended together. I felt the need to make sure that she was always taken care of. I worried that she might be catching a cold or that we might be making her walk too far. But I was always wrong. She was always front and center, her smile contagious, her capacity for love written on her sleeve. One evening I shared a story about my own grandmother with her, and she shared her stories, too. That night, she told me that she was going to be my grandmother from now on. I will never forget that.

Barbara teased me on day one. That is when I knew that I was where I belonged. Hopis and Navajos are known for their sometimes-contentious behavior and long-standing disagreements—most of it stoked by the encroachment of government on their lands. So, we loved to tease each other, and Barbara never held back. Her teases were legendary. We had the opportunity to visit Barbara's home on Hopi's Third Mesa, the Grand Canyon holding her backyard. She fed us the most delicious feast of traditional Pueblo foods, Anasazi beans, and squash. Since we both live within the same region, Barbara and I have continued to see each other from time to time and she has been one of my biggest supporters, especially on social media.

I spent a lot of time with Loretta working to document all the work she puts into her community. I journeyed with Spirit Aligned

AFTERWORD

Leadership to her home in South Dakota to watch her work on the Sun Dance ceremony in her community and had the honor of filming for her as she worked on her community projects, teaching traditional food processing to young people. She is always learning, listening to elders and to other women, to young people and their dreams. What I love most is her excitement, her love, her smile, and her laughter when she is deep in her work. You can see her dreams coming true.

Nora Naranjo-Morse and I also live remarkably close to each other in New Mexico, and I have had the immense honor of working with her on her community project. We spent hours collaborating on getting her project to convey the passion she has for passing on her knowledge to the next generation of Ohkay Owingeh. I miss her hugs and all the knowledge she carries. She taught me so much about the importance of being an artist and how that energy is to be used to light the way for all that is to become.

Jan Longboat is impeccable in her glasses, her hair perfectly braided every time, her words always perfectly rendered. When we traveled to her homelands in Ontario, we were welcomed into her home on the reserve and fed until I thought we would burst. Her home was a wonder of construction and artisanship, all built by her and her family, holding knowledge, seeds, and memories. Her work in her community—her giving voice to those in residential schools who never had a chance to speak their truth—is what makes her presence so powerful. I stopped and listened to everything she said, and I still do.

No matter how far away from Gwich'in territory we traveled, Sarah James never forgot about home. She always talked to me about home and about the work that still needed to be done. She has been a vocal activist in her homelands and is strong and intense in her advocacy. But she always remembered home, sending huge care packages back from wherever we traveled to. Her luggage was always so heavy!

In the many months we spent together, the one other camera I always saw was Yvonne's. Yvonne Peterson is a photographer, too, and we shared a quiet and observant demeanor. I like that about Yvonne. Sometimes it was just the two of us in the back of the bus, looking out the window and seeing and experiencing the beauty of where we were at that moment. She is a weaver, just like her ancestors, and her work never ends. She is always weaving a pathway for the next group of Chehalis people with her quiet reserve.

When you meet Louise Herne, you know that you are meeting power. As a Mohawk Clan Mother, she radiates love and strength and hugged me hard the first time we met. As an advocate for women in her community, she is helping the young generations to prepare for the world and making sure women are part of the dialogue. I always enjoyed moving through spaces with Louise, her laughter contagious, her love of Native jewelry moving us on in our travels.

Every single one of these Spirit Aligned Leaders has had a profound impact on me as a woman and as an artist. However, the biggest lesson I have taken away from these blessed weeks I spent with them is that I have an impact and a voice. I have a deep responsibility to create healing and to create opportunities for others within my community. We are here to help others become who they were always meant to be.

By Ramona Emerson

Diné
Author of *Shutter*

Acknowledgments

There is a whole world of people to thank for the creation of this book. The eight lives traversed and narrated are forefront, their gifts so selflessly and happily given to new generations of Indigenous people—so they may know a bit more who we are and what we are made of. I thank my husband, José Barreiro (Taíno), for his keen sense to recognize meaningful Native narrative and decades of editorial experience bringing our stories to the page. The editorial talent of my daughter-in-law, Randi Barreiro (Mohawk), who double-teamed the effort, and energetically coordinated the many sessions and interviews that supplemented other biographical materials, is also highly appreciated.

Our whole team at Spirit Aligned Leadership was important to this book. I am grateful for Gail Small (Northern Cheyenne Head Chief Woman), for providing the foreword, but I thank my sister Gail for much more, as our movement and program to recognize and support Native women elders has grown, benefiting from her tutelage to impact directly a large range of Native families and communities. I thank Ramona Emerson, emerging contemporary Native novelist, who graciously provided the afterword. The experienced publishing team of Mario Picayo and Raquel Picayo guided final design and provided excellent publishing management to take the book to press.

I acknowledge all the many elders, women and men, giant trees who guided our paths, and who kept steadfast as our traditions were buffeted and our ways of life were attacked. The spiritual shade they spread refreshes us and ushers the new generations of elders.

SPIRIT ALIGNED LEADERSHIP exists to elevate the lives, voices, and dreams of Indigenous women elders who heal, strengthen, and restore the balance of Indigenous communities.

Our goal is to honor and support Indigenous women elders who desire to intentionally transfer their knowledge and experience to younger women. Together, we identify collective wisdom and integrate solutions to help address the challenges of our times.

We are part of an emerging global movement to share our stories to gain understanding and balanced perspectives.

www.spiritaligned.org

About the Editor

TEKATSI:TSIA'KWA KATSI COOK – Onkwehonwe traditional midwife, elder, and executive director of Spirit Aligned Leadership Program, Katsi Cook is a Wolf Clan member of the Akwesasne Mohawk Nation. She resides at the St. Regis Mohawk Tribe in upstate New York. Katsi's work spans many worlds and disciplines and demonstrates a lifelong career of advancing the cultural superlatives of Indigenous knowledge. She is an advocate of Indigenous women's health across the life cycle, drawing from a longhouse traditionalist perspective the teaching, Woman Is the First Environment.

Active at the intersections of environmental reproductive health and justice, research, and policy, Katsi's body of work connected health research scientists, community health professionals, and community members. Her groundbreaking environmental research of Mohawk mother's milk revealed the harmful intergenerational impact of industrial chemicals on the health and well-being of the community. Katsi leads a movement of matrilineal awareness and rematriation in Native life. Her lifelong advocacy of Indigenous midwifery and health throughout Indigenous communities in North America continues on many fronts.

GUANI

www.ingramcontent.com/pod-product-compliance
Lightning Source LLC
Chambersburg PA
CBHW060518080526
44586CB00012B/522